more Layer Cake, Jelly Roll & Charm Quilts

more Layer Cake, Jelly Roll & Charm Quilts

Pam & Nicky Lintott

David and Charles

A DAVID & CHARLES BOOK

© F&W Media International, LTD 2011

David & Charles is an imprint of F&W Media International, LTD
Brunel House, Forde Close, Newton Abbot, TQ12 4PU, UK

F&W Media International, LTD is a subsidiary of F+W Media, Inc.
4700 East Galbraith Road, Cincinnati, OH 45236

First published in the UK and USA in 2011

Text and designs © Pam and Nicky Lintott 2011
Layout and photography © F&W Media International, LTD 2011

Pam and Nicky Lintott have asserted their right to be identified as
authors of this work in accordance with the Copyright, Designs and
Patents Act, 1988.

A catalogue record for this book is available from the British Library.

ISBN-13: 978-0-7153-3898-8 paperback
ISBN-10: 0-7153-3898-6 paperback

Printed in China by RR Donnelley
for F&W Media International, LTD
Brunel House, Forde Close, Newton Abbot, TQ12 4PU, UK

10 9 8 7 6 5 4 3 2 1

Publisher Alison Myer
Acquisitions Editors Cheryl Brown and Katy Denny
Desk Editor Jeni Hennah
Project Editor Lin Clements
Design Manager Sarah Clark
Designer Sue Cleave
Photographers Karl Adamson, Sian Irvine and Joe Giacomet
Production Manager Bev Richardson

F+W Media Inc. publishes high quality books on a wide range
of subjects. For more great book ideas visit: **www.rucraft.co.uk**

CONTENTS

INTRODUCTION

We know you enjoyed our book *Layer Cake, Jelly Roll and Charm Quilts* and we think it's time for some second helpings, so we hope you will enjoy this book as much. Working with pre-cut fabrics is such fun that we don't seem to be able to stop. Having all those fabrics pre-cut and packed up ready to sew not only speeds up the making of quilts but makes life so exciting. We know the fabrics are all going to coordinate but part of the excitement is wondering how they are going to look together when made into a quilt. Possibly you wouldn't have chosen that particular fabric, but just see how great it looks in the quilt! We don't have to go on – we love jelly rolls, layer cakes and charm packs – and we know you do too.

Having squares of fabric, as opposed to just strips, opens up many more design opportunities. Never let anyone tell you that squares are boring – you could simply sew squares

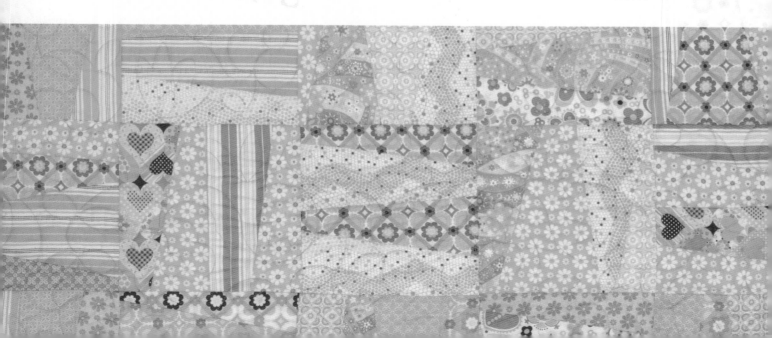

together and if you are using coordinated and inspiring fabric it would create a stunning quilt.

The 10in squares in our layer cakes gave us scope for lots of new designs. After working on our last book, *Jelly Roll Sampler Quilts*, where small units were needed for the blocks featured in the sampler quilts, the 10in squares seemed huge. We did think 'big' for some of the quilts and have made some very quick quilts which we hope you like.

Using pre-cut fabric has so many benefits – it's quick and easy and having the fabrics already coordinated means you can get straight on with a project knowing that the colours in your finished quilt are going to blend well together. Often you will be using fabrics that you wouldn't normally choose (or be brave enough to use) and we can assure you that often it is those fabrics that add the extra sparkle. We hope that this sparkle in our quilts will inspire you.

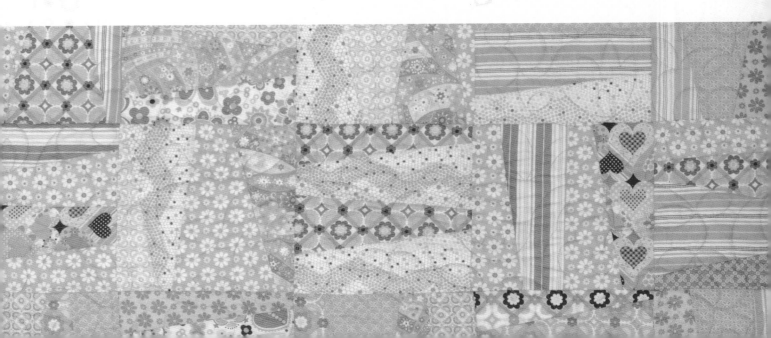

GETTING STARTED

What is a Jelly Roll™?

A jelly roll is a roll of forty fabrics cut in 2½in wide strips across the width of the fabric. Moda introduced jelly rolls to showcase new fabric ranges. How inspirational to have one 2½in wide strip of each new fabric wrapped up so deliciously! If you want to make any of the jelly roll quilts in this book and don't have a jelly roll to use, then cut a 2½in wide strip from forty fabrics from your stash and you can follow all the instructions in just the same way. Our patterns are based on a jelly roll strip being 42in long.

What is a Layer Cake™?

A layer cake is a stack of forty-two fabrics 10in square and is another brilliant way of presenting fabrics from Moda. The layer cakes used to contain only forty squares but Moda, being so customer friendly, increased it to forty-two when told that it would be more useful to have an extra two squares.

A layer cake contains approximately the same amount of fabric as a jelly roll but having the fabric in a square rather than a strip opens up some exciting design opportunities which couldn't be achieved with strips alone. If you want to make any of the layer cake quilts in this book and don't have a layer cake to use, then cut a 10in square from forty-two fabrics in your stash and you can follow all the instructions in just the same way.

What is a Charm Pack?

Historically, charm quilts are quilts in which each fabric was used only once, however small a piece it was. Only small pieces of each fabric were therefore needed so charm packs provided that need and are very useful when 'large amounts of small amounts' are required. Charm packs come in different sizes but for this book we have used the 5in charm squares that Moda produce and which are proving the most popular size.

Most charm packs contain between forty and fifty squares of fabric. We have assumed you get forty squares in a pack so, if you have more, then consider it a bonus! This also means that some of the patterns for charm packs in this book are interchangeable with layer cakes. If the pattern calls for four charm packs, you know that you can cut one layer cake into four charm packs and you will have the required amount of 5in squares.

What are Fat Eighths?

Like a fat quarter, a fat eighth is more useful than a thin one and the Busy Lizzie quilt was made with this size of pre-cut pieces. A fat quarter, which is approximately 18in x 22in, can either be cut through the 18in, making a fat eighth measurement of 9in x 22in, or through the 22in, making a fat eighth measurement of 11in x 18in. A fat eighth from a fat quarter metre will measure either 10in x 22in or 11in x 20in.

Imperial or Metric?

Jelly rolls from Moda are cut 2½in wide and at The Quilt Room we have continued to cut our strip bundles 2½in wide. Layer cakes are cut 10in square and charm squares are cut 5in. When quilt making, it is impossible to mix metric and imperial measurements. It would be absurd to have a 2½in strip and tell you to cut it 6cm to make a square! It wouldn't be square and nothing would fit.

This caused a dilemma when writing instructions for our quilts and a decision had to be made. All our instructions therefore are written in inches. To convert inches to centimetres, multiply the inch measurement by 2.54. For your convenience, any extra fabric you will need, given in the Requirements panel at the start of the quilt instructions, is given in both imperial and metric.

Seam Allowance

We cannot stress enough the importance of maintaining an accurate scant ¼in seam allowance throughout the making of a quilt. Please take the time to check your seam allowance is accurate with the seam allowance test at the back of the book, and adjust your needle position if necessary.

Quilt Size

In this book we show what can be achieved with just one jelly roll, one layer cake or four charm packs. We have sometimes added background fabric and borders but the basis of each quilt is just one – or in the case of a charm pack – just four! The size of our quilts is restricted to this fact but there is nothing to stop you using more fabric and increasing the size of your quilt. The Vital Statistics in each chapter give you all the information you need to do some simple calculations to make a larger quilt.

Diagrams

Diagrams have been provided to assist you in making the quilts and these are normally beneath or beside the relevant stepped instruction. The direction in which fabric should be pressed is indicated by arrows on the diagrams. The reverse side of the fabric is shown in a lighter colour than the right side. Read all the instructions through before starting work on a quilt.

Washing Notes

It is important that pre-cut fabric is *not* washed before use. Save the washing until your quilt is complete and then make use of a colour catcher in the wash or possibly dry clean.

GALAXY

Charm squares really are the answer to a quick quilt. When you choose fabric you love you could just sew the squares together totally at random and you would end up with a lovely quilt. With that in mind, and with just a little bit of extra work (not a lot, promise!), you could make an absolutely gorgeous quilt which looks far more complex than it really is. In this quilt the only extra work we have done is to add some snowball corners and the design is created by their clever placement next to a square of the same fabric. Sounds easy? – you bet! The quilt was made by the authors and longarm quilted by The Quilt Room.

We used charm squares in a range from French General by Moda called Maison de Garance, which combined warm reds, browns and neutrals. We chose the browns for our stars as we wanted them to stand out.

Galaxy Quilt

Vital Statistics

Finished Size:	54in x 72in
Block Size:	4½in
Blocks per Quilt:	140
Setting:	10 x 14, plus 4½in border

Requirements

- Four charm packs OR 159 5in squares
- 1yd (85cm) of fabric for borders
- 20in (50cm) of fabric for binding

SORTING YOUR SQUARES

- Choose two identical 5in squares of nineteen fabrics (i.e., thirty-eight squares) to make the nineteen stars. They need to be quite distinctive so that the stars stand out. If you haven't got identical fabrics then use squares of similar colouring.
- The remaining 121 squares will be used as background squares.

CUTTING INSTRUCTIONS

Stars:

- Take *one* square from each of the nineteen pairs of squares allocated for the stars and cut each into four 2½in squares. Keep the four 2½in squares from the same fabric together.
- Put the remaining squares from each of the nineteen pairs together in a pile for the star centres. Do *not* cut.

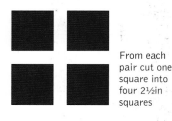 

From each pair cut one square into four 2½in squares

Leave one square uncut

Border fabric:

- Cut six 5in wide strips across the fabric width.

Binding fabric:

- Cut seven 2½in wide strips across the fabric width.

MAKING THE SNOWBALL BLOCKS

1 Draw a diagonal line from corner to corner on the wrong side of the 2½in squares allocated for the stars.

2 With right sides together, lay a marked square on a corner of one of the 5in background squares, aligning the outer edges. Sew across the diagonal, using the marked line as the stitching line. After a while you may find you do not need to draw the line but judge it by eye. Alternatively mark the line with a fold.

3 Flip the square over and press towards the outside of the block to form a snowball corner. Trim the excess fabric from the snowball corner but do not trim the background fabric. Although this creates more bulk, it helps keep the patchwork in shape.

4 Repeat with all seventy-six 2½in squares, keeping them together in their nineteen sets of four. You will only use seventy-six background squares and will have forty-five remaining. Choose background squares randomly – just make sure that the snowball corner stands out. By the end of this step you should have nineteen sets of four snowball blocks, nineteen star centres and forty-five background squares.

Nineteen sets of four snowball blocks

Nineteeen star centres

Forty-five background squares

ASSEMBLING THE QUILT

5 Lay out all your charm squares in fourteen rows of ten, referring to the diagram, right, to see the placement. Make sure you have the correct star centre to match the four snowball blocks. When you are happy that everything is in the correct place, sew the squares into rows and then sew the rows together, pinning at every seam intersection to ensure a perfect match.

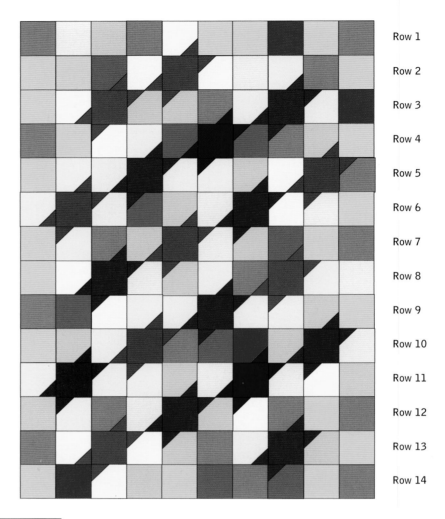

Row 1
Row 2
Row 3
Row 4
Row 5
Row 6
Row 7
Row 8
Row 9
Row 10
Row 11
Row 12
Row 13
Row 14

ADDING THE BORDER

6 Join your border strips together to form a long length. Determine the vertical measurement from top to bottom through the centre of your quilt top. Cut the two side borders to this measurement, sew them to the quilt and press seams.

7 Now determine the horizontal measurement from side to side across the centre of the quilt top. Cut two borders to this measurement, sew to the quilt and press seams.

8 Your quilt top is now complete. Quilt as desired and bind to finish – see Quilting and Binding a Quilt.

You can imagine this delicate floral quilt thrown over a chair or sofa to add a country-cottage effect to a room. This range of florals called Dream On, from Moda, also contained soft stripes and we picked these out for our stars, which created a much softer effect. The quilt was made by the authors and longarm quilted by The Quilt Room.

HIDDEN TREASURE

The nine-patch block has got to be the original 'transformer' – it can turn itself into something completely different with ease. With four charm packs and some additional fabric you have a single-size bed quilt in no time. For our main quilt we used a neutral marble as our additional fabric but as you can see from our variation at the end of this chapter you can ring the changes by adding a selection of fabrics instead of just one. You can also play around with the blocks by using different placement and rotation to create further variations. Do experiment as there are certainly lots of design options here. The quilt was made by the authors and longarm quilted by The Quilt Room.

The background fabric we chose for this quilt was a neutral Moda marble to coordinate with our charm squares, a Three Sisters range called Park Avenue, which had a lovely selection of blues, reds and browns.

Hidden Treasure Quilt

Vital Statistics

Finished Size:	60in x 72in
Block Size:	6in
Blocks per Quilt:	120
Setting:	10 x 12

Requirements

- Four charm packs OR 144 5in squares
- 2¼yd (2.10m) of additional fabric for the large triangles
- 24in (60cm) of fabric for binding

SORTING YOUR SQUARES

- This quilt starts out as sixteen nine-patch blocks. The fabric placement in the blocks is important.
- Choose sixteen darks for the centres of the nine-patch blocks. This makes the distinctive brown squares shown in our quilt.
- Choose sixty-four mediums for the corners of the nine-patch blocks.
- Choose sixty-four lights for the remaining squares.

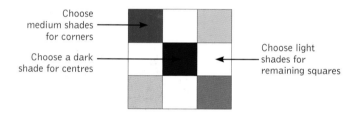

Choose medium shades for corners

Choose a dark shade for centres

Choose light shades for remaining squares

CUTTING INSTRUCTIONS

Blocks:
- Cut eleven 7in strips across the width of the additional fabric and subcut each strip into six 7in squares. You need sixty-four in total – two are spare.

Binding fabric:
- Cut seven 2½in wide strips across the fabric width.

MAKING THE NINE-PATCH BLOCKS

1 Sew nine squares together, placing the lights, mediums and darks as shown. Press the work. Repeat to make sixteen nine-patch blocks.

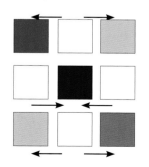

2 Working with one nine-patch block at a time, cut one block accurately through the centre in each direction as shown to make four quarters. The centre segment is 4½in wide so the best method of cutting accurately is to line up the 2¼in mark on your ruler on the seam line.

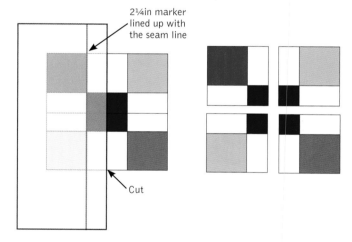

2¼in marker lined up with the seam line

Cut

3 On the reverse of one of these quarters, mark the diagonal line from light corner to light corner. Make sure you do not mark through the dark square.

4 Lay this unit, right sides together, on top of a 7in background square aligning the edges. Pin to hold in place. Sew either side of the marked diagonal line with a seam allowance no larger than a scant ¼in.

5 Cut along the marked diagonal line and press as shown to reveal two different blocks.

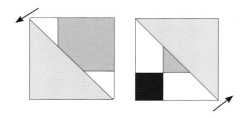

6 Lay a quilting square over each block to check it measures 6½in, trimming if necessary. If your blocks are under 6½in then your seam allowance when sewing either side of the diagonal marked line (step 4) is too large. Move the needle position on your machine to the right to make your seam allowance slightly narrower. You can always trim the excess but you don't want blocks too small.

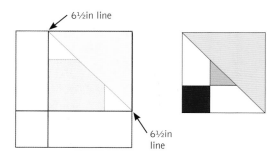

7 Repeat with the other three quarters of the nine-patch block to make a further six blocks.

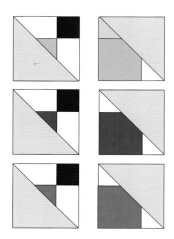

8 Repeat steps 2–7 with the remaining fifteen nine-patch blocks to create a total of 128 blocks. You need 120, so eight will be spare.

ASSEMBLING THE QUILT

9 Referring to the diagram below, lay out the blocks into twelve rows of ten. When you are happy with the layout, sew the blocks into rows and then sew the rows together. Press the seams of alternate rows in opposite directions so the seams nest together nicely.

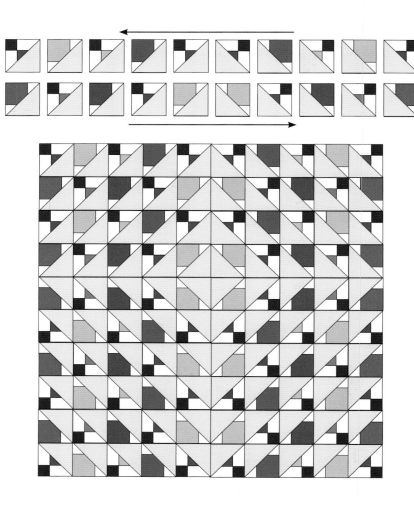

10 Your quilt top is now complete. Quilt as desired and bind to finish – see Quilting and Binding a Quilt.

In our variation instead of adding just one additional fabric for our large triangles we used different coloured fat quarters to create a very jolly quilt. If you wish to do the same, instead of 2¼yd (2.10m) of one fabric, you need eleven fat or long quarters and cut each quarter into six 7in squares – sixty-four in total. The quilt was made by the authors and longarm quilted by The Quilt Room.

CHARMING WINDMILLS

In our book *Layer Cake, Jelly Roll and Charm Quilts* we kept all our charm quilts as squares, just adding a touch extra to create an exciting design. We decided in this book to be more adventurous and this lovely quilt features a windmill block, which creates a nice sense of movement. The quilt does require an accurate seam allowance so maybe now is a good time for a re-check. Yes, we hear your groans but a few minutes now could save you lots of groans later! We used four identical charm packs which meant that we had four identical charm squares to work with, all in beautiful salmon pink and chocolate shades, with touches of blue and green.

If you don't have four identical charm squares to put together then choose squares with similar colouring – your quilt will just be a little bit scrappier! You could of course use a layer cake and cut each 10in square into four 5in squares.

Charming Windmills Quilt

Vital Statistics

Finished Size:	51in x 51in
Block Size:	7in square
Blocks per Quilt:	36
Setting:	6 x 6 + 4½in wide border

Requirements

- Four charm packs OR 144 5in squares
- 30in (75cm) of border fabric
- 20in (50cm) of fabric for binding

SORTING YOUR CHARM SQUARES

- This design works best with four identical dark squares and four identical light squares in each block so your first sorting is to collect up the identical squares from your four packs. Some blocks can be scrappy so don't panic if this is not always possible.
- Pair up a group of four dark squares with a group of four light squares and put in separate piles. You need eighteen piles.

CUTTING INSTRUCTIONS

Border:
- Cut five 5in wide strips across the fabric width.

Binding:
- Cut six 2½in wide strips across the fabric width.

MAKING THE WINDMILL BLOCKS

1 Working with one pile of fabric squares at a time, mark the diagonal on the *reverse* of the four light squares.

2 Pair up the four light squares with the four dark squares, right sides together and ensuring all edges are aligned. Pin to secure.

3 Sew either side of the marked line with an accurate scant ¼in seam allowance. Cut along the marked line of each pair to create eight half-square triangle units. Trim the dog ears and press to the dark fabric. You will have eight units.

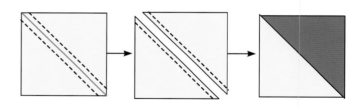

4 Rotate four of the units so that the dark triangle is top left and rotate four units so that the dark triangle is bottom left. This positioning is very important. Your squares should measure 4½in. If not, adjust your seam allowance.

Rotate 4
this way

Rotate 4
this way

5 Each square has to be cut in half and the easiest way to do this is to use the 2¼in marker on your ruler aligned with the left edge of the squares. This will mean that you are cutting down the centre.

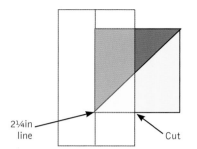 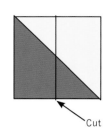

2¼in line

Cut

Cut

6 You now have sixteen rectangles with a light or dark triangle at one end. These need to be trimmed to measure 2¼in x 4in but you **must not** trim the end with the triangle.

 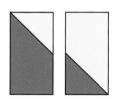

7 Turn all your rectangles so that the triangle is on the left and using the 4in marker on your ruler, trim to 4in. Repeat with all sixteen rectangles.

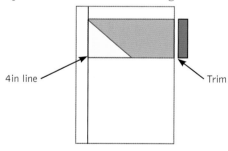

4in line

Trim

8 Sew two rectangles with dark triangles as shown. Repeat to make four of these. Press the work.

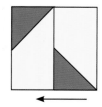

9 Sew two rectangles with light triangles as shown. Repeat to make four of these. Press the work.

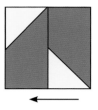

10 Sew the units with dark triangles together to make one light block. Press the work.

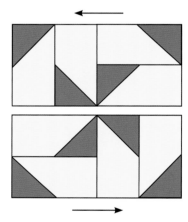

11 Sew the units with light triangles together as shown to make one dark block. Press the work as shown.

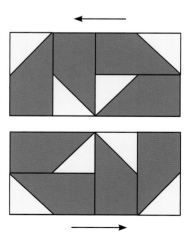

12 Repeat with your other piles of squares to make eighteen light blocks and eighteen dark blocks in total.

13 Lay out your blocks, alternating a dark block with a light block. When you are happy with the arrangement, sew the blocks into rows, pinning at every seam intersection. Press the seams of alternate rows in opposite directions so that they will nest together nicely. Sew the rows together pinning at every seam intersection to ensure a perfect match.

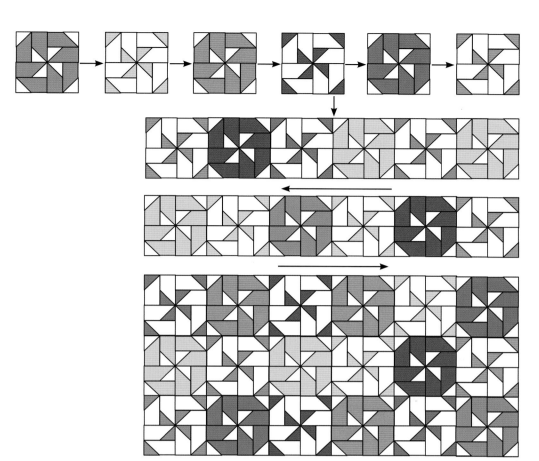

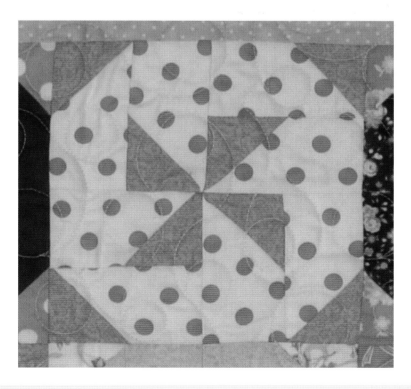

ADDING THE BORDER

14 Determine the vertical measurement from top to bottom through the centre of your quilt top. Cut two side borders to this measurement. Pin and sew to the quilt and press.

15 Join the remaining three border strips into one continuous length. Determine the horizontal measurement from side to side across the centre of the quilt top. Cut two borders to this measurement. Sew to the top and bottom of your quilt and press.

16 Your quilt top is now complete. Quilt and bind as desired – see advice in Quilting and Binding a Quilt.

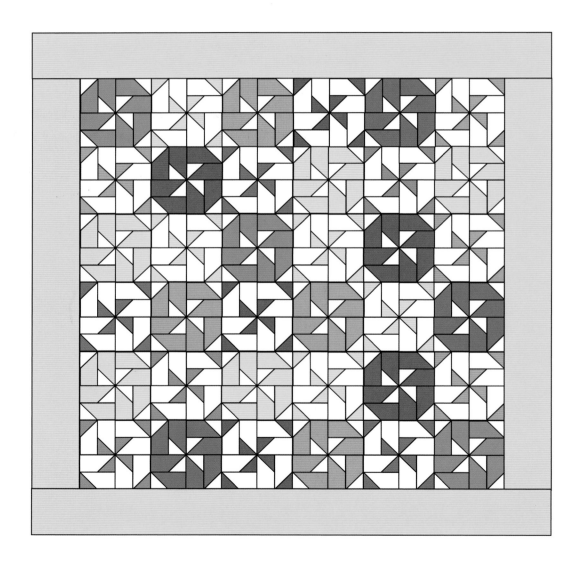

In our black and white variation we used just two charm packs and cut the rest of the squares needed from our own choice of a white tone-on-tone fabric. If you plan to do the same you will need 1⅓yds (1.25m) of light fabric cut into seventy-two 5in squares. The quilt was made by Ellen Seward and longarm quilted by The Quilt Room.

FOUR-PATCH FLIP

The secret of success with this quilt is being sufficiently bold with your additional fabric. You need to make the stars surrounding the dark four-patch blocks stand out. It is also important to have contrast between the dark and light four-patch blocks, so look out for suitable charm packs with a good selection of lights and darks. You could also use two charm packs in a medium/dark range of fabrics plus two plain/neutral charm packs. We carried the pattern into the border which didn't make too much extra work and really enhanced the overall design.

We fell in love with this range by Brannock & Patek called Lilac Hill with its gorgeous combination of lilacs, greens and reds. It also had lots of great lights and was the perfect choice for this pattern. We decided on black for our additional fabric which ensured that our stars showed up well.

Four-Patch Flip Quilt

Vital Statistics

Finished Size:	54in x 72in
Block Size:	9in
Blocks per Quilt:	35
Setting:	5 x 7, plus 4½in border

Requirements

- Four charm packs OR 140 5in squares
- 1¼yd (1.10m) of accent fabric for snowball corners
- 1yd (90cm) of fabric for borders
- 20in (50cm) of fabric for binding

SORTING THE SQUARES

- Sort the squares into seventy-two dark squares and sixty-eight light squares.
- Divide the dark squares into eighteen piles of four to make the dark four-patch blocks. We chose to have four different fabrics in each block but kept them with similar colouring, although you can have them as scrappy as you like.
- Divide the light squares into seventeen piles of four to make the light four-patch blocks.

CUTTING INSTRUCTIONS

Snowball corners:
- Cut fifteen **2¾in** wide strips across the width of the accent fabric. Subcut each strip into fifteen **2¾in** squares to make 225 in total. Nine are spare. (Sorry to stress the 2¾in but we are all so used to cutting 2½in wide strips we don't want any mistakes!)

Border fabric:
- Cut six 5in wide strips across the fabric width.
- Subcut five strips into ten rectangles 5in x 18½in and four squares 5in x 5in.
- Subcut one strip into four rectangles 5in x 9½in.

Binding fabric:
- Cut seven 2½in wide strips across the fabric width.

MAKING THE DARK FOUR-PATCH BLOCKS

1 Draw a diagonal line from corner to corner on the wrong side of a 2¾in square.

2 With right sides together, lay a marked square on a corner of one of the 5in dark squares, aligning the outer edges. Sew across the diagonal, using the marked diagonal line as the stitching line. After a while you may find that you do not need to draw the line but judge it by eye. Alternatively, mark the line with a fold.

3 Flip the square over and press towards the outside of the block to form a snowball corner. Trim the excess fabric from the snowball corner but do not trim the dark fabric. Although this creates more bulk, it helps keep your patchwork in shape.

4 Repeat with all seventy-two dark squares, keeping them together in their eighteen sets of four.

Make 18 sets of dark squares

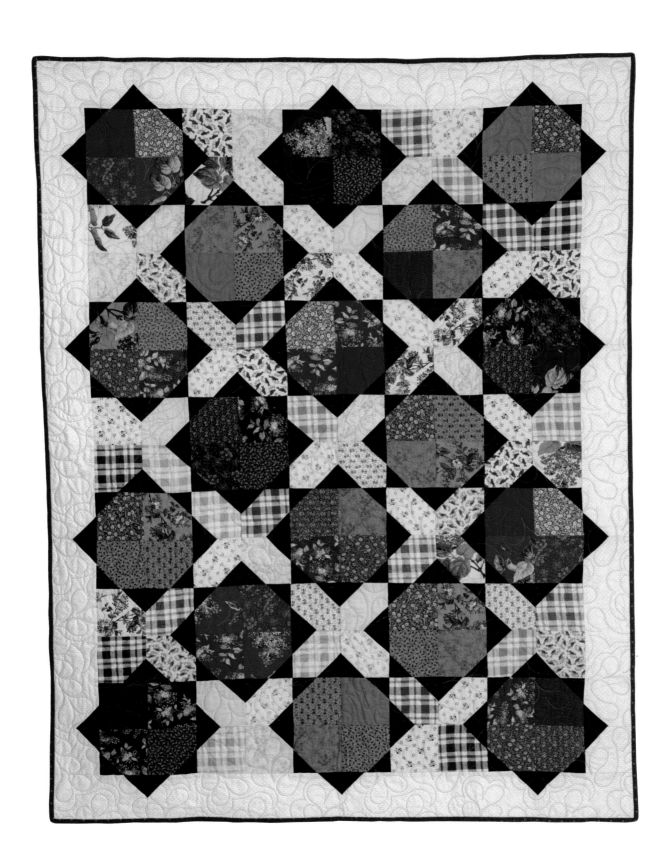

5 Sew the squares from each pile into a four-patch block making sure the snowball corners are on the outside of the block as shown. Press the work. Make eighteen dark four-patch blocks.

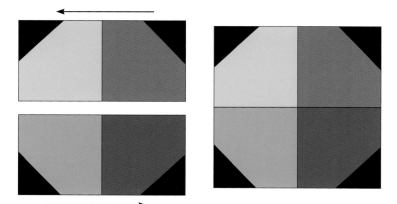

Make 18

MAKING THE LIGHT FOUR-PATCH BLOCKS

6 Repeat steps 1–4 to create seventeen piles of light squares with one snowball corner on each.

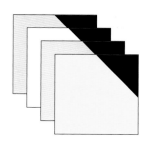

Make 17 sets of light squares

7 Take seven piles of light squares and sew a second snowball corner on the diagonally opposite corner of every square as shown. Sew the squares together to form seven light four-patch A blocks. Press the work.

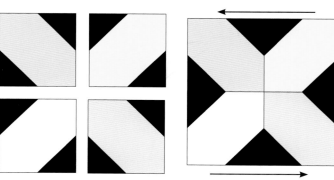

Make 7 light A blocks

8 Take the remaining ten piles of light squares and sew a second snowball corner on the diagonally opposite corner of *only two of the squares* in each pile. Sew the squares together as shown to form ten light B four-patch blocks.

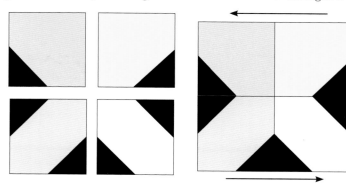

Make 10 light B blocks

ASSEMBLING THE QUILT

9 Referring to the diagram below, lay out the blocks, making sure you rotate the light B blocks where necessary. When you are happy with the layout sew the blocks into rows and then sew the rows together. Press the seams of alternate rows in opposite directions so that the seams nest together nicely when sewn together. Press the work.

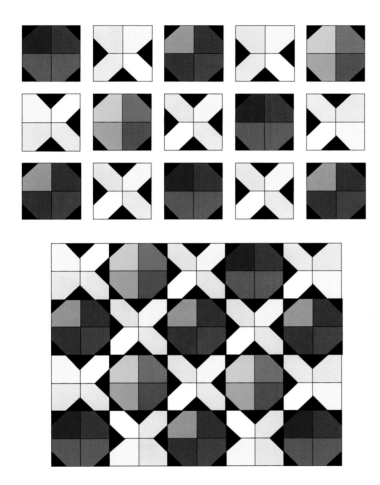

MAKING THE BORDER

10 Sew a snowball corner to each end of the ten 5in x 18½in rectangles. Press the work.

Make 10

11 Sew a snowball corner to one corner of the four 5in border squares. Press the work.

Make 4

12 Sew a snowball corner to one corner of the four 5in x 9½in rectangles as shown.

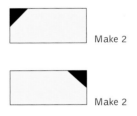

Make 2

Make 2

13 Join the two side borders together as shown below. Join the top and bottom borders as shown. Press the work.

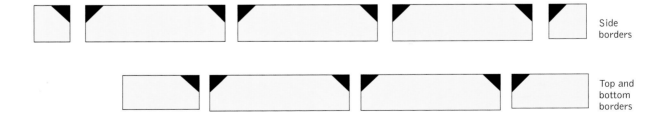

Side borders

Top and bottom borders

14 Pin and sew the side borders to each side of the quilt, pinning and easing where necessary. Press the work. Pin and sew the top and bottom borders to the quilt, pinning and easing where necessary. Press the work.

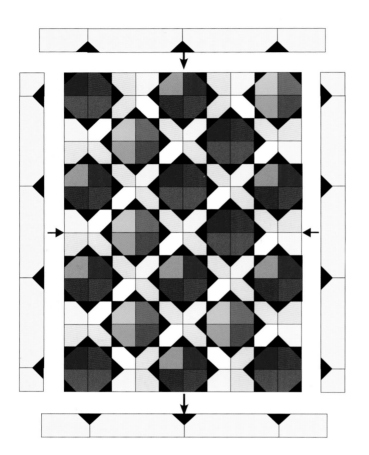
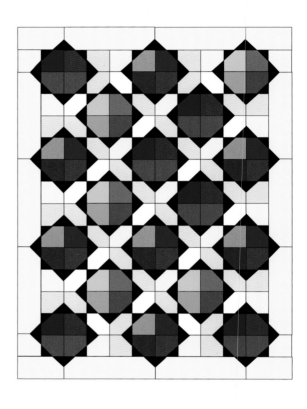

15 Your quilt top is now complete. Quilt as desired and bind to finish – see Quilting and Binding a Quilt.

For this variation of the quilt we used a stylish Moda range called Fandango, where the contrast between the light and dark fabrics is sufficient for the pattern to work. The bright orange we chose for the stars is bold and stands out well. The quilt was made by the authors and longarm quilted by The Quilt Room.

HIGH FASHION

This unusual design makes good use of the large squares in a layer cake and is a very quick quilt to make. The slowest part for us was hand appliquéing the bag handles, although the finished effect is great. You could of course use machine appliqué, which would speed things up immensely. The quilt is made up of twenty handbag blocks, simply framed with a dark binding. Each quilt will look unique as the shape of the bags will vary slightly and the handles can be appliquéd to form different curves. You could also create the quilt in quite different fabrics, making your bags as bright and bold as you like — see the colourful variation quilt at the end of this chapter.

The layer cake used for this quilt is a subtle range from Three Sisters called Luna Notte, which has a slight Japanese look to it. We just loved the pale aqua mixed with the dusty pink, which has given a classic look to the quilt.

High Fashion Quilt

Vital Statistics

Finished Size:	43in x 61in
Block Size:	8½in x 14in
Blocks per Quilt:	20
Setting:	5 x 4 blocks

Requirements

- One layer cake OR forty-two 10in squares
- 20in (50cm) of fabric for binding

SORTING YOUR SQUARES

- Select thirteen of the lightest squares for the background rectangles.
- Select twenty squares for the bags.
- Select four squares for the handles.
- Five squares are spare.

CUTTING INSTRUCTIONS

Background:
- Take the thirteen light squares for the background rectangles and cut them in half so each measures 5in x 10in. Trim them to create twenty-six rectangles 5in x 9in. You need twenty-five, so one is spare.

Binding fabric:
- Cut six 2½in wide strips across the fabric width.

MAKING THE BAG BLOCKS

1 Start by pairing up the squares for the bags. Each pair will make two bag units. In one bag unit, one fabric will form the centre of the bag unit and the second fabric will be the background. In the second bag unit this will be reversed.

2 Working with one pair at a time, layer the two together, both *right sides up* aligning edges. Make two cuts across in the shape of a bag, as shown. There is no need for any measuring – just cut where you think it looks good. The cuts will vary when you cut the other layers which will make the bag blocks slightly different and make the quilt look more effective.

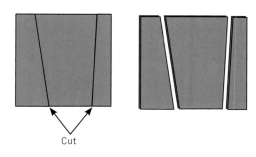

Cut

3 Separate the pieces into two units, taking the fabric piecing from each centre section and swapping them, so you have two units in opposite colours, as shown.

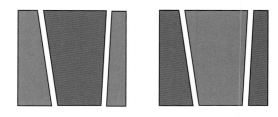

4 Sew the first three pieces together to make your first bag unit. Repeat with the second bag unit. Repeat the process with all ten pairs of bag squares to make a total of twenty bag units.

MAKING THE HANDLES

5 Take the four squares allocated for the handles and layer them together, right sides up, aligning the edges. Press to hold in place.

6 You now need to cut 1in bias strips from these squares. The easiest way to do this is to lay the ½in marker of your quilting ruler across the diagonal of the squares and rotary cut ½in from the diagonal line. Then, using the 1in marker, make two further cuts 1in apart. Rotate the bottom section and measuring from the cut edge cut three more 1in strips to make a total of five strips. You will now have twenty 1in wide bias strips of varying lengths from your four fabrics for your bag handles.

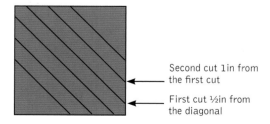

Second cut 1in from the first cut

First cut ½in from the diagonal

7 Take one bag handle strip and position it on the ironing board, wrong side up. Fold and gently press one long side in and then fold and gently press the other long side in, so the sides meet or nearly meet in the middle of the strip.

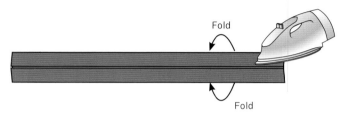

Fold

Fold

8 To position the handle on a 5in x 9in background rectangle, have the bottom basket section available so you can match up the handle and the bag. Position the right-hand side of the handle in place with the tip of the iron and then, holding the bias strip in your left hand (or vice versa if you are left-handed), continue to press with the iron while you gently stretch the handle into position. The bias cutting will help the fabric strip stretch and ease into position.

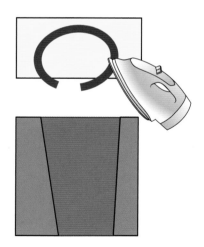

9 When in position, secure with pins and either hand or machine appliqué into position – see panel below for hand appliqué. Press the finished handle. As some of your bias strips are longer than others, the handles will all be slightly different, which brings additional interest.

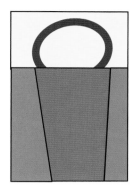

10 With right sides together, sew the handle section to the bag section to complete your first bag block. Repeat to make twenty bag blocks in total.

WORKING HAND APPLIQUÉ

To hand stitch the appliqué handles in place, use a small invisible hemming stitch from the fold of the appliqué straight down into the background and returning to the fold about ¼in further on. Use either invisible thread or thread the colour of the appliqué rather than the colour of the background fabric.

FINISHING YOUR QUILT

11 Lay out your blocks into vertical rows with the remaining 5in x 9in background rectangles placed at the bottom of rows 1, 3 and 5 and at the top of rows 2 and 4, as shown in the diagram below.

Row 1   Row 2   Row 3   Row 4   Row 5

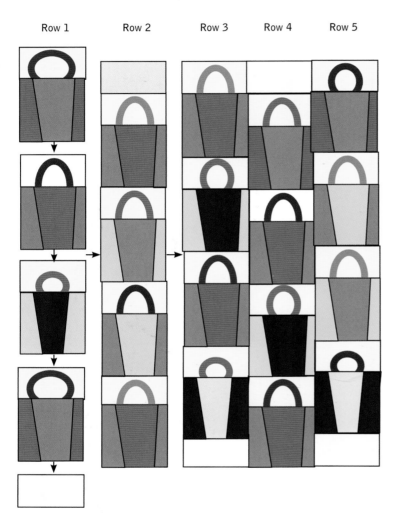

12 When you are happy with the arrangement, sew the blocks into vertical rows. Press the seams of alternate rows in opposite directions so they will nest together nicely.

13 Sew the rows together pinning at every seam intersection to ensure a perfect match and then press.

14 Your quilt top is now complete. Quilt and bind as desired – see advice in Quilting and Binding a Quilt.

Our variation is made up in a range called Happy by Me and My Sister for Moda, and the fabrics really live up to their name. Ellen Seward made the quilt, piecing the top in only two hours. She then spent the next day appliquéing the handles – so it really is a quick one to make. The quilt was longarm quilted by The Quilt Room.

TUMBLERS

This is a great pattern for showcasing fabrics you love because the blocks are large, which means you can leave it up to the fabrics to speak for themselves. Yes, you could just sew squares together but see how much more interesting you can make it look by creating tumbler shapes and sewing them together. It takes a small amount of effort and the results are certainly worth it. You could make this quilt in totally different fabrics to stunning effect – Japanese taupes would look great, as would a large, modern print for a very trendy look. The quilt was made by the authors and longarm quilted by The Quilt Room.

The layer cake used for this quilt is a bold, bright and beautiful range from Lecien called Flower Sugar, which we absolutely loved. You really can let this fabric speak for itself.

Tumblers Quilt

Vital Statistics

Finished Size: 54in x 78in
Blocks per Quilt: 42
Setting: 7 x 6, plus 6in border

Requirements

- One layer cake OR forty-two 10in squares
- 1¼yd (1.10cm) of border fabric
- 20in (50cm) of binding fabric

CUTTING INSTRUCTIONS

Layer cake squares:
- Make a mark along the top of one of the layer cake squares 2in from each side.

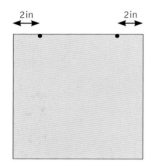

- With your rotary cutter and ruler cut from the bottom right-hand corner to the 2in mark on the right-hand side as shown in the diagram. Alternatively, if you have a marked cutting board you can position the layer cake on the board so that the markings on the board show you where the 2in mark is and you can use this instead of marking the fabric.

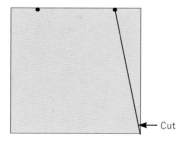

- Repeat on the left-hand side, cutting from the bottom left-hand corner to the 2in mark on the left side. The offcuts are spare.

- Repeat to cut all your forty-two layer cake squares into tumbler-shaped blocks. You can stack your layer cake squares for speed but be careful not to lose accuracy.

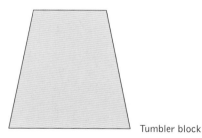

Tumbler block

Border fabric:
- Cut six 6½in wide strips across the fabric width.

Binding fabric:
- Cut six 2½in wide strips across the fabric width.

JOINING THE TUMBLER BLOCKS

1 Lay a tumbler block right side up. Lay a second tumbler right side up next to the first tumbler and rotate the second tumbler 180 degrees.

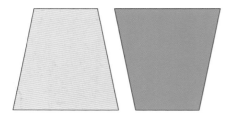

2 Flip the second tumbler on top of the first, right sides together. Pin and sew to join the tumblers. The fabrics need to match at the point where you start sewing and at the point where you finish sewing, so you will find the corner points appear slightly out. Open and press the work.

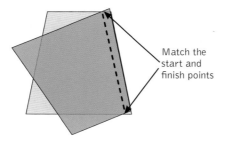

Match the start and finish points

3 Repeat by sewing a third tumbler the same way up as the first tumbler and repeat until you have six tumblers sewn together. Press the seams in one direction, as shown.

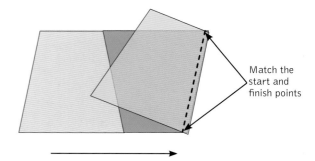

Match the start and finish points

4 Repeat to make seven rows of six tumblers each, as shown. Press the seams of alternate rows in opposite directions so they nest together when sewing the rows together. Sew the rows together, pinning at every seam intersection to ensure a perfect match, and then press.

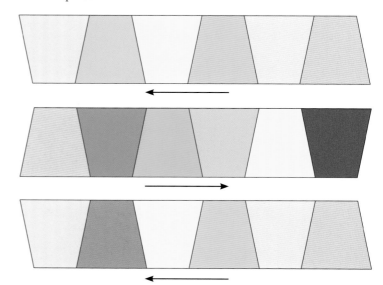

ADDING THE BORDERS

5 Join your border strips together to form a continuous length. Determine the vertical measurement from top to bottom through the centre of your quilt top. Cut the two side borders to this measurement. Pin and sew to the quilt to form a straight edge and then press.

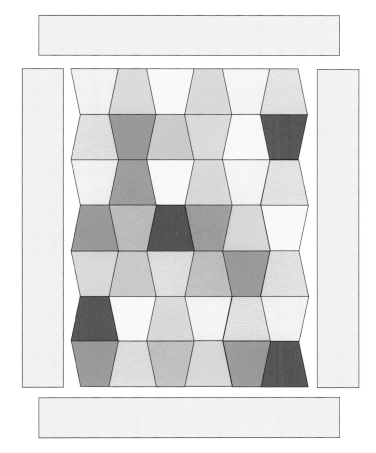

6 Determine the horizontal measurement from side to side across the centre of the quilt top. Trim two borders to this measurement, sew to the quilt and press.

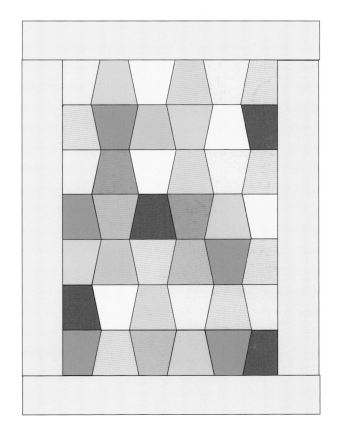

7 Your quilt top is now complete. Quilt as desired and bind to finish – see Quilting and Binding a Quilt.

TIPSY TUMBLERS

Instead of a variation for Tumblers we decided to do something a bit different and here we have Tipsy Tumblers. This quilt uses the method of stack, slice, shuffle and sew, and speeds together in no time at all. When we started this quilt we just meant to do a block to see how it would look but before we knew it, the quilt was finished. It's a fun quilt to make and is really easy to put together once you get into the rhythm of working with the fabric piles. It would look great in just about any combination of colours. The quilt was made by the authors and longarm quilted by The Quilt Room.

This range from Moda's Minnick & Simpson contains the all-time favourite companions of red, white and blue, and it's hard to go wrong with this combination.

Tipsy Tumblers Quilt

Vital Statistics

Finished Size: 54in x 54in
Block Size: 18in
Blocks per Quilt: 9
Setting: 3 x 3

Requirements

- One layer cake OR forty-two 10in squares
- 20in (50cm) of binding fabric

SORTING THE SQUARES

- Sort the squares into nine piles of four squares, each consisting of two light and two dark. Our piles contained one navy, one red for our darks and then two lights. Six squares are spare.

CUTTING INSTRUCTIONS

Binding fabric:
- Cut six 2½in wide strips across the fabric width.

MAKING THE BLOCKS

1 Working with one pile at a time, layer the four squares in the pile *right side up*, alternating the dark and the light fabrics. Ensure all the edges are aligned and press to hold in place.

2 Measure accurately 4½in left from the top right corner and make a small mark, as shown in the next diagram, and then measure 4½in down from the top right corner and make a small mark.

3 Repeat in the bottom left corner, making marks 4½in up from the bottom left corner and 4½in right of the bottom left corner.

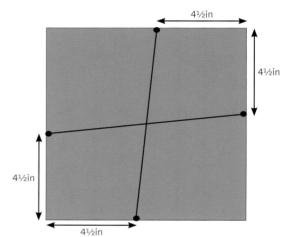

4 Cut your pile of squares into four quarters using these marks as your guides. We have labelled our quarters clockwise A, B, C and D although you don't need to label.

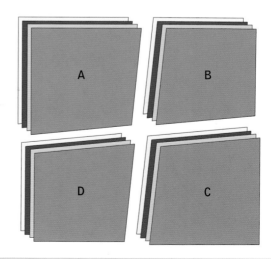

5 Now that you have stacked and sliced your fabrics it is time to shuffle your fabric piles as follows.
A – leave the pile unchanged.
B – put the top fabric to the bottom of the pile.
C – put the top two fabrics to the bottom of the pile.
D – put the top three fabrics to the bottom of the pile.

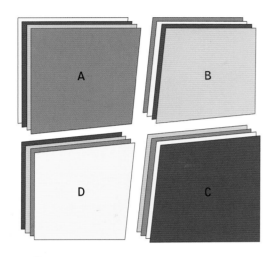

6 Take the top A, B, C and D fabrics and sew them together, pinning at every seam intersection to form a square and ensuring outer edges are aligned. Take extra care aligning the centre seams. Press as shown.

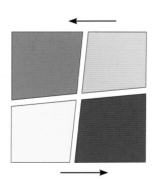

7 Repeat to make four squares. Two will have large dark quarters with smaller light quarters and two will have large light quarters with smaller dark ones.

8 Rotate the blocks so that large quarters of each of the four fabrics are together in the centre of the block. There are a couple of ways your block can look. We aimed to have our dark fabrics lined up diagonally, to give a diagonal run of colour throughout the quilt. The important thing is that the large quarters are next to the large quarters and the small quarters are next to the small quarters so all seams match up. Sew the quarters together, pinning at every seam intersection and then press as shown.

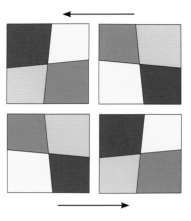

9 Your first block is now complete. Repeat this process to make a total of nine blocks.

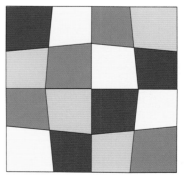

Make
9 blocks
in total

ASSEMBLING THE QUILT

10 Lay out your blocks and when you are happy with the arrangement, sew the blocks into rows, pinning at every seam intersection. Press the seams of alternate rows in opposite directions so that they will nest together nicely. Sew the rows together pinning at every seam intersection to ensure a perfect match.

11 Your quilt top is now complete. Quilt as desired and bind to finish – see Quilting and Binding a Quilt.

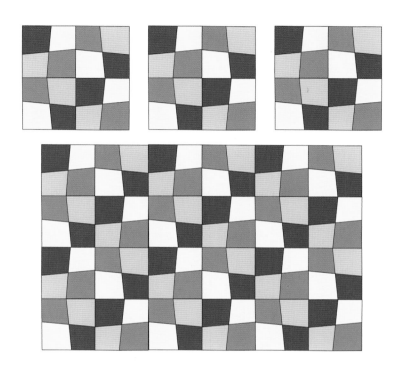

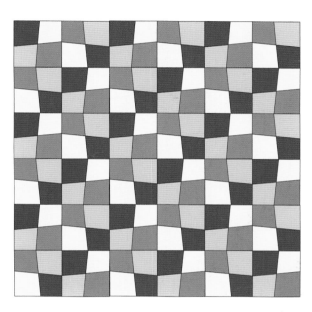

SIMPLICITY

We loved the effect of this simple pattern. It is important to choose a layer cake that has sufficient contrast between the light and dark fabrics but apart from that anything goes. It is such a quick and easy quilt to make, with virtually no seams to match and very little pinning. It would be a great quilt to make for a loved one heading off to college or moving away for the first time – you know that at least they will stay warm! A bonus cushion was made from the cut off triangles – there's something very satisfying in making something from scraps that would have been thrown away! The quilt and cushion were made by the authors and longarm quilted by The Quilt Room.

Our layer cake for this easy quilt was a lovely range of Japanese taupe fabrics which had lots of super lights to mix with the greys and browns combined with a burst of dark red.

Simplicity Quilt

Vital Statistics

Finished Size:	48in x 74in
Block Size:	2½in x 16in
Blocks per Quilt:	60
Setting:	15 x 4, plus 5in border

Requirements

- One layer cake OR forty 10in squares
- 1yd (1m) of border fabric
- 20in (50cm) of binding fabric

SORTING THE LAYER CAKE

- Divide the layer cake into twenty light and twenty dark squares.

CUTTING INSTRUCTIONS

Layer cake:

- Cut each layer cake into three rectangles 3in x 10in. You can stack three or four at a time, aligning the edges carefully, to speed up cutting.

- Take each 3in x 10in rectangle and using either a ruler with a 45 degree marking or a 45 degree triangle, make a 45 degree cut, starting at the bottom right corner. You need sixty light and sixty dark triangles. See our bonus cushion before throwing offcuts away!

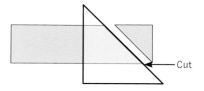

Border fabric:

- Cut six 5½in wide strips across the fabric width.

Binding fabric:

- Cut seven 2½in wide strips across the fabric width.

MAKING THE UNITS

1 Take one dark unit and one light unit and with right sides together sew together along the 45 degree cut. Note that when sewing units with angled cuts, they appear to be ¼in out at each end. It is important to check that your edges are straight so check the alignment after sewing your first two units together.

2 Press towards the dark fabric. Repeat with all sixty light and dark units.

3 Lay out the units starting at the top left with the dark at the top and rotating alternate units 180 degrees. When you are happy with the layout sew the units into rows and then sew the rows together pinning at every seam intersection to ensure a perfect match. Press the work.

ADDING THE BORDERS

4 Determine the horizontal measurement from side to side across the centre of the quilt top. Trim two borders to this measurement, sew to the top and bottom of the quilt and press. Sewing these borders on first means you do not have a join in them.

5 Determine the vertical measurement from top to bottom through the centre of your quilt top. Join two border strips and trim to this measurement. Sew to one side of the quilt. Repeat on the other side. Press the work.

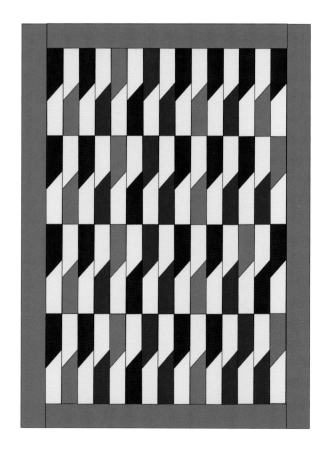

6 Your quilt top is now complete. Quilt as desired and bind to finish – see Quilting and Binding a Quilt.

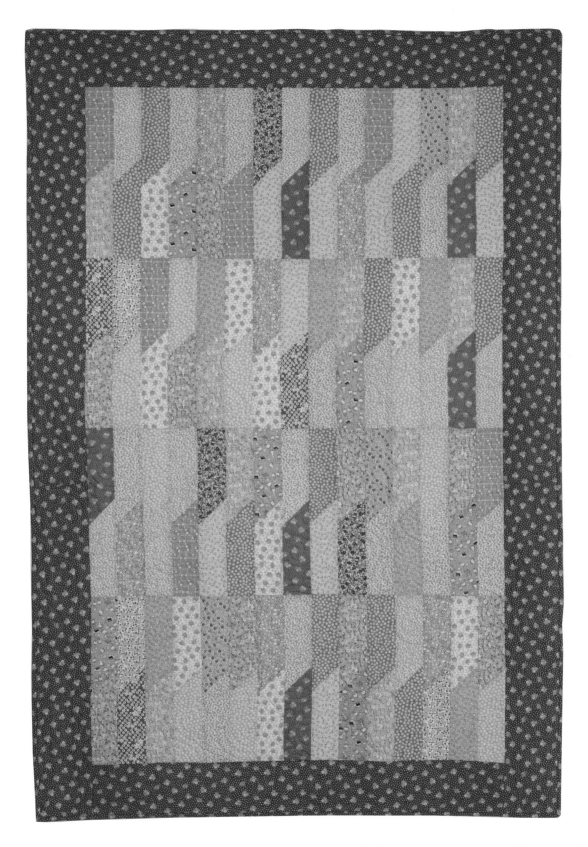

Thirties reproduction fabrics always look so fresh and bright and although there wasn't quite so much contrast between the lights and the darks in this fabric range it made a beautiful quilt. The quilt was made by Vivian de Lang and was longarm quilted by The Quilt Room.

Triangles Cushion

Vital Statistics

Finished Size:	18in x 18in
Unit Size:	2in x 2in
Units per Cushion:	49
Setting:	7 x 7, plus 2in border

Requirements

- Forty-nine light and forty-nine dark triangles, offcuts from the Simplicity Quilt
- Two strips 2½in x 14½in and two strips 2½ x 18½in for borders
- Two pieces 18½ x 15in for cushion back
- Cushion pad 18in (46cm) square

MAKING THE CUSHION FRONT

1 Pair up the light and dark triangles. Sew the pairs together by chain piecing along the diagonals. Cut off the dog ears, open and press to the dark fabric to make forty-nine half-square triangle units.

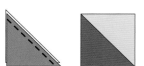

2 Lay out the units into a setting of seven by seven. Sew the units together to form one row and then sew the rows together, pinning at every seam intersection to ensure a perfect match. Press the work.

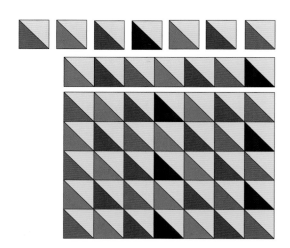

3 Pin and sew the two 2½in x 14½in borders to the sides of the cushion and press. Pin and sew the two 2½in x 18½in borders to the top and bottom of the cushion and press. Quilt your cushion top if desired.

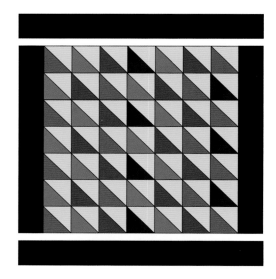

MAKING UP AN ENVELOPE CUSHION

4 Hem one long end of each backing piece. With right sides together lay both backing pieces on to the pieced top and pin in place. They will overlap by about 4in. Sew the seams using a generous ¼in seam allowance. Turn the cushion cover right sides out, insert your pad through the gap in the back and your cushion is complete.

DANCING STARS

A layer cake is perfect for making this quilt as it saves so much time and gives you the variety of fabrics needed. At first we were going to cut our layer cake squares into 3¼in squares so there would be less wastage – we just can't help ourselves – but in the end decided on 3in squares and had to accept the small amount of fabric not used! The dancing stars are formed from flip-over corners made from different sized squares. It is a really fun quilt to make as your stars become quite personal to you. The quilt was made by the authors and longarm quilted by The Quilt Room in the ever popular Maggie's Rose design.

We used some of Lecien's gorgeous Japanese flower fabrics in rich dark colours as our layer cake. Our border of black seemed the perfect choice to finish to the quilt, adding a dramatic contrast colour to the layer cake shades.

Dancing Stars Quilt

Vital Statistics

Finished Size: 51in x 58½in
Block Size: 7½in
Blocks per Quilt: 42
Setting: 6 x 7, plus 3in borders

Requirements

- One layer cake OR forty 10in squares
- 1yd (1m) of fabric for star points
- 24in (60cm) of border fabric
- 20in (50cm) of binding fabric

SORTING THE FABRICS

Star points:

- Cut six 2½in wide strips across the width of the fabric and subcut each strip into sixteen 2½in squares. You need eighty-four in total, so twelve will be spare.
- Cut eight 2in wide strips across the width of the fabric and subcut each strip into twenty-one 2in squares. You need 168 in total.
- Cut three 1½in wide strips across the width of the fabric and subcut each strip into twenty-eight 1½in squares. You need 84 in total.

Border fabric:
- Cut six 3½in wide strips across the width of the fabric.

Binding fabric:
- Cut six 2½in wide strips across the width of the fabric.

MAKING THE BLOCKS

1 Cut each layer cake square into nine 3in squares and keep them together in piles. Repeat with all forty-two squares. You will find that by layering the squares and aligning the edges you can cut a number of squares at the same time but do not cut too many at once or you will lose accuracy. The offcut strips are spare.

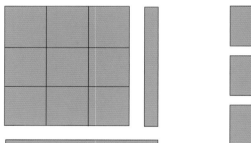

2 Working with one pile of nine 3in squares at a time, take one 2in star point square and lay it right sides together on one of the 3in squares. Sew across the diagonal. If it helps, draw the diagonal line in first or make a fold to mark your stitching line. Flip the square over and press towards the light fabric. Trim the excess light fabric but do not trim the 3in square. Although this creates more bulk, it helps to keep your work in shape. Repeat by sewing a 2in star point to one corner of four 3in squares.

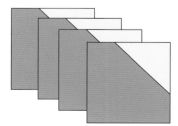

3 Take two of these squares and sew a 1½in star point square as shown, pressing and trimming as before.

4 Take the other two squares and sew a 2½in star point square as shown. Do not sew across the diagonal on the 2½in square as you want to create a long point. Mark a line from approximately the centre of one side to one corner and follow this as your sewing line. This line can vary, to individualize the stars.

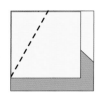

5 Flip the square over and press towards the light fabric as before.

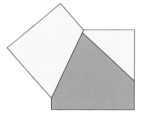

6 Turn the square to the reverse and using a rotary cutter and ruler trim the excess light fabric from the square.

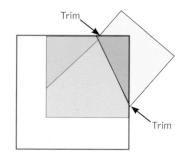

7 Take the four squares with star points and sew them together with the remaining squares from the pile as shown. Press seams in the directions shown.

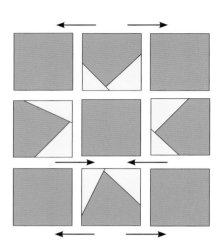

8 Repeat with all forty-two piles of layer cake
squares to make forty-two blocks.

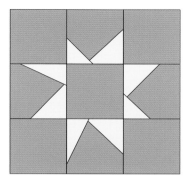

ASSEMBLING THE QUILT

9 Lay out your blocks and when you are happy with
the arrangement, sew the blocks into rows, pinning at
every seam intersection. Press the seams of alternate rows
in opposite directions so that they will nest together nicely.
Sew the rows together pinning at every seam intersection to
ensure a perfect match. Press the work.

ASSEMBLING THE BORDER

10 Join the border strips into a continuous length. Determine the vertical measurement from top to bottom through the centre of your quilt top. Cut two side borders to this measurement. Pin and sew to the quilt and press the work.

11 Determine the horizontal measurement from side to side across the centre of the quilt top. Cut two borders to this measurement. Sew to the top and bottom of your quilt and press the work.

12 Your quilt top is now complete. Quilt as desired and bind to finish – see Quilting and Binding a Quilt.

After using the darker Lecien fabrics in our main quilt we decided to stay with the Lecien fabrics and made our variation in the delicate Durham range. The quilt was made by the authors and longarm quilted by The Quilt Room.

BUSY LIZZIE

We have been using fat eighths for a while at The Quilt Room and a few years ago we used this pattern to make a wedding quilt for a friend. This is a quick and easy quilt which uses a method of stack, slice, shuffle and sew to create the 8in blocks. It is easy to increase the size by using more fat eighths. The technique used in this quilt is perfect for fat eighths and it doesn't matter whether you are using fat eighth yards or fat eighth metres – the pattern works well with either. The blocks are made up of angle-cut pieces and this creates a lovely scrappy feel to the quilt. An all-over quilting pattern in a floral motif completes the flower theme.

Moda have introduced lovely big bundles of fat eighths to showcase their new ranges. In this quilt we have used fat eighths from a pretty range by Anna Griffin called the Lizzie Collection – hence the name of this quilt.

Busy Lizzie Quilt

Vital Statistics

Finished Size:	48in x 56in
Block Size:	8in square
Blocks per Quilt:	42
Setting:	6 x 7

Requirements

- Twenty-one fat eighths (fat eighth yards or metres are both fine)
- 20in (50cm) of fabric for binding

SORTING YOUR FABRICS

- The technique requires stacking fabrics in groups of four in a variety of colours but this sorting should be done *after* step 1 below.

CUTTING INSTRUCTIONS

Binding fabric:

- Cut six 2½in wide strips across the fabric width.

MAKING THE BLOCKS

1 Take each fat eighth and cut in half to form forty-two rectangles measuring approximately 9in x 10in. This measurement will vary slightly but don't trim any to size.

2 Take four rectangles in a variety of colours and with *right sides facing up* stack them on top of each other. The narrower sides should be placed top and bottom, and the top and side edges should be aligned as much as possible. The bottom edges might not match exactly but do not worry about this. Press to hold in place.

3 With your rotary cutter make three cuts across the fabrics similar to the diagram to create four segments. These slices are random and no measuring is required to cut them in the correct place. Whatever you choose is the right place!

 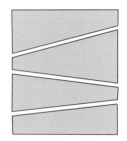

4 We have labelled our segments A, B, C and D but you do not need to label yours. Shuffle the segments as follows.
A – leave unshuffled.
B – move the top layer to the bottom of the pile.
C – move the top two layers to the bottom of the pile
D – move the top three layers to the bottom of the pile.

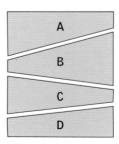

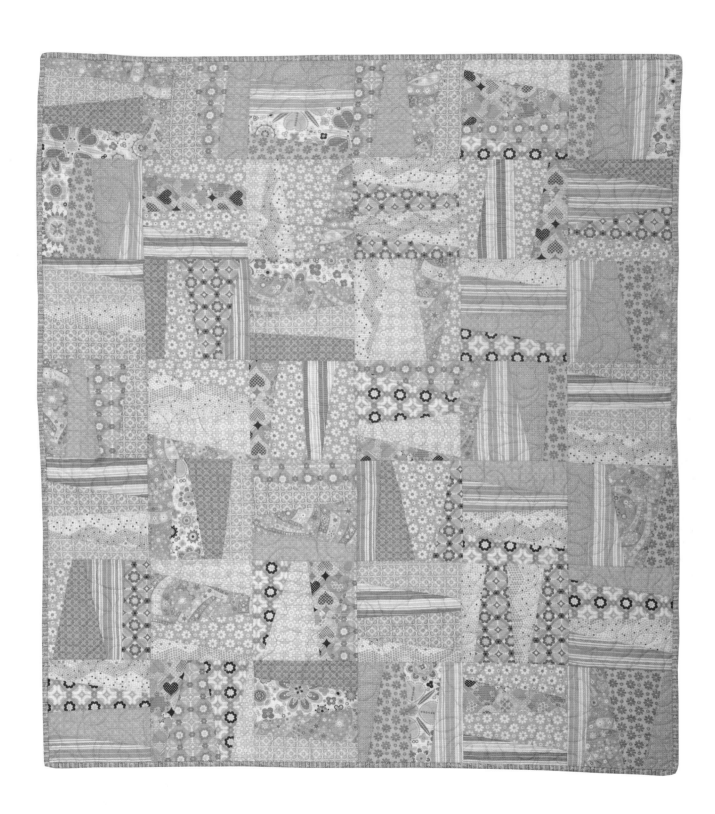

5 Your top rectangle will now look like the diagram below. Sew the segments in the top rectangle together to form a block with the four segments all different fabrics, making sure the edges are aligned.

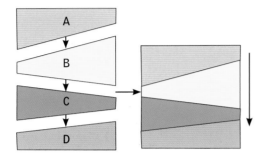

6 Sew the other three rectangles together. Press the seams in one direction. Do not trim at this stage as you will need to trim all your squares to the same measurement.

7 Repeat by stacking, slicing, shuffling and sewing another four rectangles and continue until all your rectangles are used. Your last two rectangles can be stacked with just two together. You will end up with a total of forty-two blocks. Your slicing can be different for each stack to give more variation to your quilt.

8 Measure the shortest side of the smallest block and using a quilter's square trim all the blocks square to this measurement. Our shortest side was 8½in so we trimmed all our blocks to measure 8½in square. Your measurement may vary but the important thing is that all your blocks are the same size.

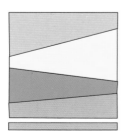

9 Lay out your blocks into seven rows of six blocks each, rotating alternate blocks 90 degrees. When you are happy with the layout, sew the blocks into rows. Press the seams of alternate rows in opposite directions so that they will nest together nicely (shown by long arrows on the diagram below). Sew the rows together pinning at every seam intersection to ensure a perfect match. Press the work.

10 Your quilt top is now complete. Quilt as desired and bind to finish – see Quilting and Binding a Quilt.

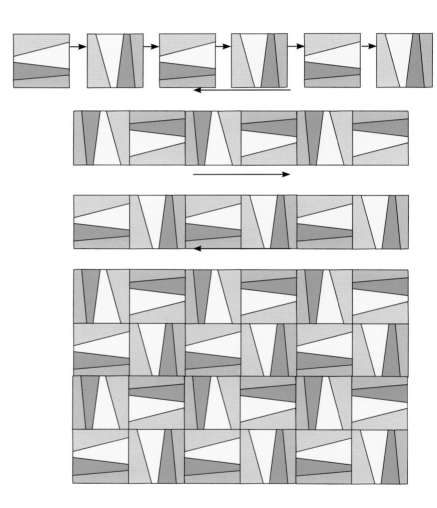

Our variation quilt was made from Moda's Luna Notte range. These delicate Japanese-looking fabrics, with their lovely colouring of dusty pink, aqua, grey and black, create a totally different effect. The quilt was made by Vivienne Ridgeway and longarm quilted by The Quilt Room.

HEXAGON GARDEN

So many spectacular designs can be created with a 60 degree triangle and here we have used just about every inch of a gorgeous French General jelly roll to make this quilt. The pattern is created by sewing the triangle units together into half hexagon units, which are then combined in vertical lines. This means there are no set-in seams required to join the hexagons. It is a really simple quilt to make but you do need a bit of space to lay out the design before sewing it all together to avoid mistakes. You will also be working with bias edges so remember, gentle pressing only! We chose the blue floral fabric from the jelly roll for the border fabric, which ties it all together beautifully.

The jelly roll we used for this quilt was a lovely red, white and blue one from French General called Rural Jardin. The bright reds give just the right splash of colour to the quilt.

Hexagon Garden Quilt

Vital Statistics

Finished Size:	51in x 53in
Setting:	8 vertical rows plus 3in wide border

Requirements

- One jelly roll OR forty 2½in strips cut across the width of the fabric
- 20in (50cm) of border fabric
- 20in (50cm) of binding fabric
- 60 degree triangle ruler

SORTING YOUR STRIPS

- Divide the jelly roll strips into thirteen sets of three strips. Each set of three strips will make one hexagon so you can choose how you want them to look. We tried to have two strips of similar colours for the outside of the hexagon and a light or dark for the centre strip in each set. Be guided by what is in your jelly roll. One strip is spare.

CUTTING INSTRUCTIONS

Border fabric:
- Cut five strips 3½in wide across the fabric width.

Binding fabric:
- Cut six strips 2½in wide across the fabric width.

MAKING THE TRIANGLE UNITS

1 Take one set of three strips and sew them together to form a strip unit as shown. Press the seams in one direction. Repeat to make thirteen strip units.

2 Working with one strip unit at a time, take the 60 degree triangle ruler and place on the left side of the strip unit. Place the triangle as far to the left as possible as you need to cut nine triangles from each unit. Align the 6½in line of the triangle with the bottom of the unit and align the cut-off top of the triangle with the top of the unit. Cut your first triangle.

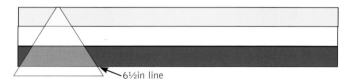

6½in line

3 Rotate the ruler 180 degrees and cut the second triangle. Continue to the end to cut nine triangles.

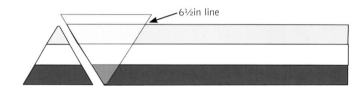

6½in line

4 You will have two different triangles – five of one and four of the other. Keep them all together in one pile. Repeat with the other strip units to make thirteen piles of triangles.

JOINING THE TRIANGLE UNITS

5 Find some space to lay out the triangles into hexagons as shown (see also next diagram). Select six triangles from each pile, three of each type, and lay them out to form a hexagon, alternating the segments. The remaining three triangles in each pile will be used to make the fourteenth hexagon, the half hexagons and used to fill the gaps around the edges of the quilt.

6 Make the fourteenth hexagon scrappy by choosing triangles from the remaining triangles in the piles. Lay out the hexagons as shown.

7 Once you have decided on the placement of the hexagons you can then lay out the four half hexagons and use the remaining triangles to fill in the gaps around the edges.

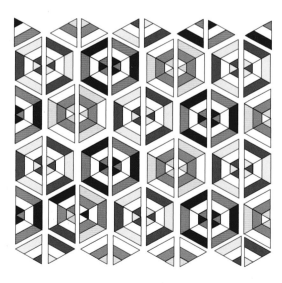

8 Sew the triangles together in vertical rows starting with the top left and sewing one row at a time. Pin at every seam intersection to ensure a perfect match. Press all seams in the first row *up* and all seams in the second row *down*. There are bias edges so press gently.

9 Sew the vertical rows together pinning at every seam intersection. Press the work.

ADDING THE BORDER

10 Rotate your quilt top 90 degrees so the top of the quilt is now on the top. Join your border strips into one continuous length. Determine the vertical measurement from top to bottom through the centre of your quilt top. Join and cut two side borders to this measurement. Pin and sew to the quilt to form a straight edge. Press and trim the excess fabric.

11 Determine the horizontal measurement from side to side across the centre of the quilt top. Cut two borders to this measurement. Sew to the top and bottom of your quilt and press.

12 Your quilt top is now complete. Quilt and bind as desired – see advice in Quilting and Binding a Quilt.

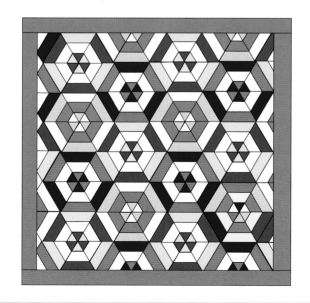

For this variation quilt, a dark, rich country effect is created with this reproduction range called Looking Back, by Linda Brannock for Moda, which contains lush blacks, golds, greens and reds. The quilt was made by the authors and longarm quilted by The Quilt Room.

TWISTED BRAID

Who would have thought that this complex-looking quilt is made from one simple unit comprising two squares and one rectangle, but it is! We loved Moda's Lily & Will range by Bunny Hill Designs, with its apple greens, pale blues and dusty pinks, but when we saw that the jelly rolls had been split into three different colourways, we had a dilemma! A brave decision was taken and we jumbled up all three jelly rolls and just picked forty strips! We really loved the end result and I hope you agree that it was worth a bit of a cheat. The quilt was made by the authors and longarm quilted by The Quilt Room.

In our variation quilt at the end of this chapter we not only used just one jelly roll but did absolutely no sorting of fabrics. So if you have a jelly roll that doesn't lend itself to our pattern's split of colours then just make all the blocks using your strips randomly. Your quilt will look just as gorgeous.

Twisted Braid Quilt

Vital Statistics

Finished Size: 64in x 76in
Block Size: 8in
Blocks per Quilt: 28
Setting: 4 vertical rows with 3in sashing, plus 3in border

Requirements

- One jelly roll OR forty 2½in strips cut across the width of the fabric
- 1¾yd (1.60m) of fabric for light squares and setting triangles
- 2yd (1.85m) of sashing, border and binding fabric

SORTING THE JELLY ROLL STRIPS

- Colour A (blue) – choose six strips to be colour A.
- Colour B (green) – choose five strips to be colour B.
- Colour C (brown) – choose thirteen strips to be colour C.
- Colour D (pink) – choose thirteen strips to be colour D.
- Three strips are spare.

CUTTING INSTRUCTIONS

Colour A (blue):
- Take four strips and cut each into eight rectangles 2½in x 4½in. You need thirty-two in total.
- Take two strips and cut each into sixteen squares 2½in x 2½in. You need thirty-two in total.

Colour B (green):
- Take three strips and cut each into eight rectangles 2½in x 4½in. You need twenty-four in total.
- Take two strips and cut each into sixteen squares 2½in x 2½in. You need twenty-four. Eight are spare.

Colour C (brown):
- Take seven strips and cut each into eight rectangles 2½in x 4½in. You need fifty-two. Four are spare.
- Take two strips and cut each into sixteen 2½in x 2½in squares. You need twenty-eight. Four are spare.
- Leave four strips uncut.

Colour D (pink):
- Take seven strips and cut each into eight rectangles 2½in x 4½in. You need fifty-two. Four are spare.
- Take two strips and cut each into sixteen 2½in x 2½in squares. You need twenty-eight. Four are spare.
- Leave four strips uncut.

Background and setting triangle fabric:
- Cut eight 2½in strips across the fabric width.
- Cut five 7½in strips across the fabric width. Subcut each strip into five 7½in squares. You need twenty-four 7½in squares.
- Cut across both diagonals of the 7½in squares to form ninety-six triangles. Cutting the triangles this way ensures there are no bias edges on the outside.

Sashing and border fabric:
- Cut seven 3½in strips *lengthways* down the fabric – three are for sashing strips and four are for borders.
- Cut four 2½in strips *lengthways* down the fabric for the binding.

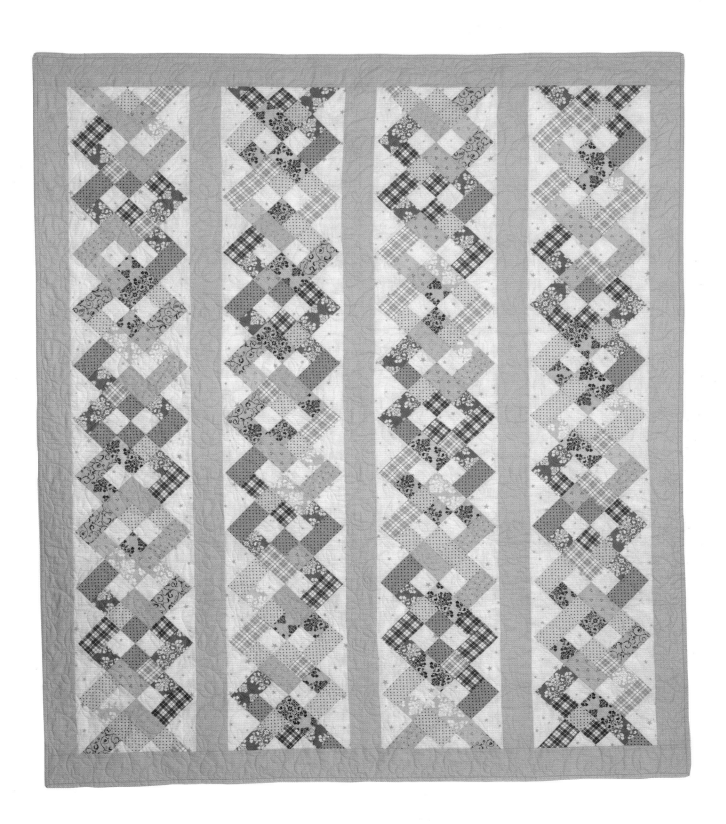

MAKING THE BLOCKS

1 With right sides together sew a colour A square to a colour C square as shown. Press the work. Make sixteen.

2 With right sides together sew this unit to the left side of a colour A 2½in x 4½in rectangle to make Unit A1. Press the work. Repeat to make sixteen Unit A1.

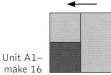

Unit A1– make 16

3 With right sides together sew a colour A square to a colour D square. Press the work. Make sixteen.

4 With right sides together sew this unit to a colour A 2½in x 4½in rectangle to make Unit A2. Press the work. Repeat to make sixteen Unit A2.

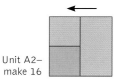

Unit A2– make 16

5 With right sides together sew a colour B square to a colour C square. Press the work. Make twelve.

6 With right sides together sew this unit to the left side of a colour B 2½in x 4½in rectangle to make Unit B1. Press the work. Make twelve Unit B1.

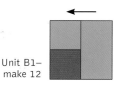

Unit B1– make 12

7 With right sides together sew a colour B square to a colour C square. Press the work. Make twelve.

8 With right sides together sew this unit to the left side of a colour B 2½in x 4½in rectangle to make Unit B2. Press the work. Make twelve Unit B2.

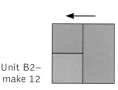

Unit B2– make 12

9 Take one colour C strip and one 2½in background strip and sew together. Press towards the darker fabric and then subcut into sixteen 2½in segments. Repeat with the other three colour C strips and three 2½in background strips. You need fifty-two segments in total – twelve are spare.

10 With right sides together sew one of these units to the left side of a colour C 2½in x 4½in rectangle. Make fifty-two in total.

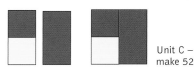

Unit C – make 52

11 Take one colour D strip and one 2½in background strip and sew together. Press towards the darker fabric and subcut into sixteen 2½in segments. Repeat with the other three colour D strips and three 2½in background strips. You need fifty-two segments in total – twelve are spare.

12 With right sides together sew one of these units to the left side of a colour D 2½in x 4½in rectangle. Make fifty-two in total.

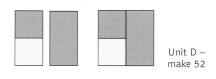

Unit D – make 52

ASSEMBLING THE BLOCKS

13 Sew two Unit A1s to two Units Cs, to create a C1 block, pinning at every seam intersection to ensure a perfect match. Make eight C1 blocks.

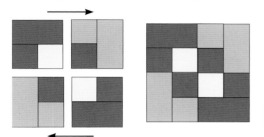

Block C1 – make 8

14 Sew two Unit A2s to two Units Ds, to create a D1 block, pinning at every seam intersection to ensure a perfect match. Make eight D1 blocks.

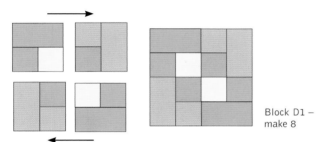

Block D1 – make 8

15 Sew two Unit B1s to two unit Cs, to create a C2 block, pinning at every seam intersection to ensure a perfect match. Make six C2 blocks.

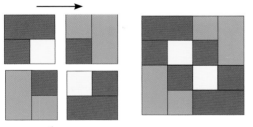

Block C2 – make 6

16 Sew two Unit B2s to two unit Ds, to create a D2 block, pinning at every seam intersection to ensure a perfect match. Make six D2 blocks.

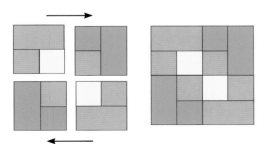

Block D2 – make 6

MAKING THE SETTING TRIANGLE UNTS

17 Sew a setting triangle to either side of twenty-four Unit Cs, aligning the edges of the setting triangles as shown. Press the work.

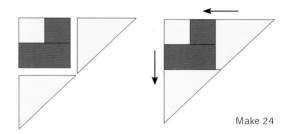

Make 24

18 Sew a setting triangle to either side of twenty-four unit Ds, aligning the edges of the setting triangles as shown. Press the work.

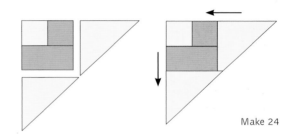

Make 24

ASSEMBLING THE VERTICAL ROWS

19 Sew a setting triangle unit to *one* side of block C1, aligning the edges as shown and pinning at the seam intersections. Press the work. Make four. Repeat to make four using block D1.

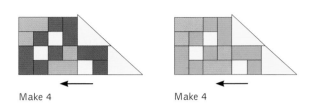

Make 4   Make 4

21 Sew a setting triangle unit to *both* sides of block C2, aligning the edges as shown and pinning at each seam intersection. Press the work. Make six. Repeat to make six using block D2.

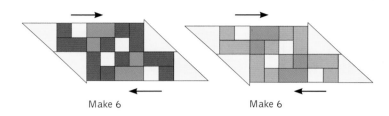

Make 6   Make 6

20 Sew a setting triangle unit to *both* sides of block C1, aligning the edges as shown and pinning at each seam intersection. Press the work. Make four. Repeat to make four using block D1.

Make 4   Make 4

22 Sew the blocks together as shown, alternating the colours to form one vertical row, pinning at every seam intersection to ensure a perfect match. Make two rows starting with a C1 block and two rows starting with a D1 block.

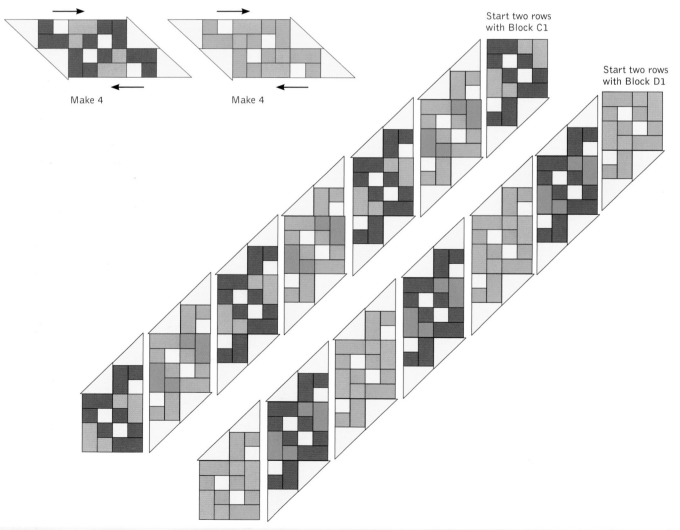

Start two rows with Block C1

Start two rows with Block D1

SEWING THE SASHING AND SIDE BORDERS

23 Once your segments are sewn into vertical rows measure them all from Point A to Point B (see diagram right). They should all be the same but you never know!

24 Trim three sashing strips and two side borders to this measurement plus ½in. It is important that the sashing strips all measure the same. It is better to allow an inch or so extra, which can be trimmed later, than cut these sashing strips too short.

25 When attaching sashing and side borders to a vertical row, first pin the centre and ends of both the sashing and the vertical row together. You can then pin the rest, easing the strips if necessary.

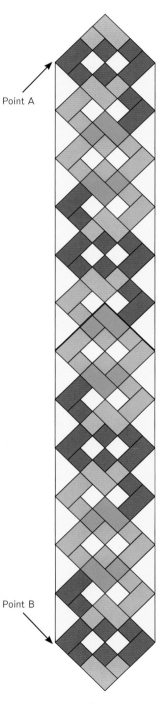

Point A

Point B

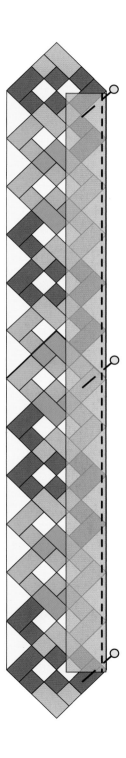

26 Sew the sashing strips and the side borders to the vertical rows. Press towards the sashing strips and borders. Sew the vertical rows together.

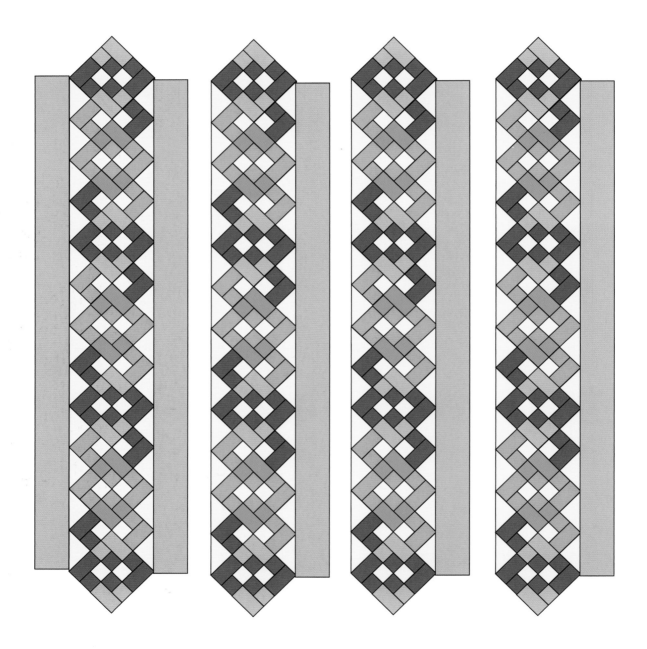

ADDING THE TOP AND BOTTOM BORDERS

27 Determine the horizontal measurement from side to side across the centre of the quilt top and trim the two borders to this measurement. Pin and sew to the top and bottom of the quilt, trim the excess fabric and press.

28 Your quilt top is now complete. Quilt as desired and bind to finish – see Quilting and Binding a Quilt.

MAKING THE VARIATION QUILT

If you are not sorting your fabrics these notes will simplify the making of the units.

- Start by taking twenty jelly roll strips and cut each into eight rectangles 2½in x 4½in. You will need 160 in total.
- Take eight jelly roll strips, pair them up and sew into four strip units. Cut fifty-six 2½in segments.
- Sew a 2½in x 4½in rectangle to these segments to make a total of fifty-six assorted units.

Make 56 assorted units

- Sew seven jelly roll strips to seven background strips and cut the strip units into 104 2½in segments. Sew a 2½in x 4½in rectangle to these segments, making sure the background square is always at bottom left.

Make 104 units with the background square at bottom left

- All other instructions are the same as the main quilt.

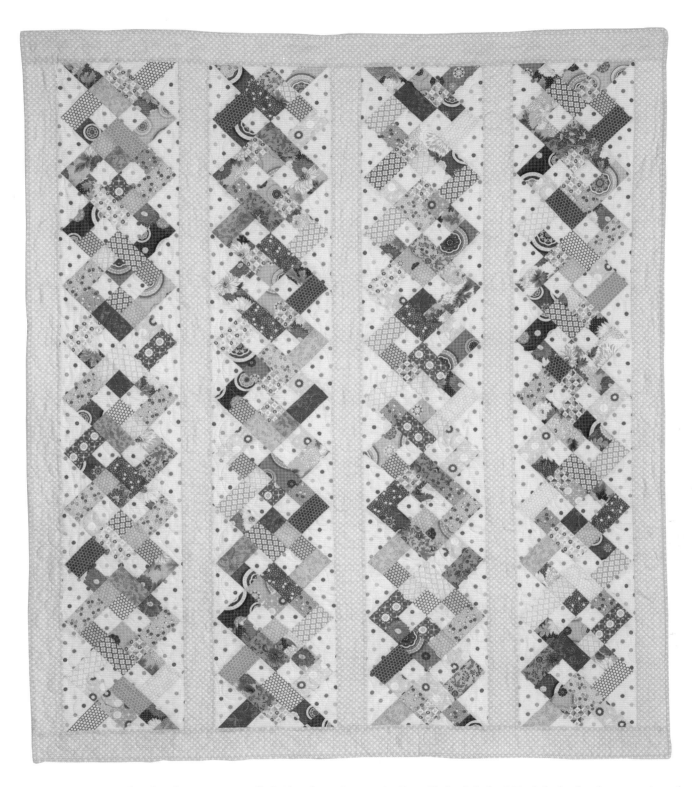

Our variation uses a bright, cheery range called Bliss from Bonnie & Camille for Moda. We did absolutely no sorting of fabrics and used whatever fabric came to hand. The braid doesn't stand out quite so much when the fabrics aren't sorted but combined with the multicoloured dot fabric from Lecien it makes a fun quilt. The quilt was made by the authors and longarm quilted by The Quilt Room.

DOUBLE NINE-PATCH

A simple nine-patch block is given a new twist in this pretty quilt. We have added sashing and sashing squares and when the blocks and sashing are sewn together another nine-patch block is formed. So if you love nine-patch blocks as much as we do you will enjoy making this quilt. The nine-patch block has been such a favourite over many, many years that it seemed appropriate to use a thirties reproduction fabric plus a crisp white-on-white to create a really fresh and vibrant quilt. The quilt was made by the authors and longarm quilted by The Quilt Room.

For this quilt we used a jelly roll with a lovely combination of 1930s reproduction fabrics, combined with a crisp white-on-white fabric for the sashing and flip-over corners.

Double Nine-Patch Quilt

Vital Statistics

Finished Size:	50in x 62in
Block Size:	10in
Blocks per Quilt:	20
Setting:	4 x 5 blocks, plus 2in sashing

Requirements

- One jelly roll OR forty 2½in strips cut across the width of the fabric
- 1¾yd (1.6m) of fabric for sashing and flip-over corners
- Binding from jelly roll strips

SORTING THE STRIPS

- Choose twenty strips to make the nine-patch frame in each block.
- Choose fourteen strips and put into seven pairs to make the nine-patch blocks.
- The remaining six strips will be used for binding.

CUTTING INSTRUCTIONS

Jelly roll strips:
- Take the twenty jelly roll strips allocated for the frames and cut each strip into:
  four rectangles 2½in x 6½in, keeping them together in piles;
  five squares 2½in x 2½in. This will make 100 (110 are needed and the ten extra will be obtained from the offcuts from the nine-patch blocks).
- Leave the fourteen strips allocated for the nine-patch blocks uncut.

Sashing fabric:
- Cut twenty-three 2½in wide strips across the width of the fabric.
- Take ten of these strips and subcut each strip into sixteen 2½in squares for the flip-over corners. You need 160.
- Take the remaining thirteen strips and subcut into four rectangles 2½in x 10½in for the sashing. You need forty-nine in total. Three are spare.

MAKING THE NINE-PATCH BLOCKS

1 Take one pair of strips and trim the selvedge. Cut each strip into three lengths of 14in.

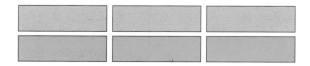

2 From your six lengths assemble two strip units. Press seams towards the darker fabric.

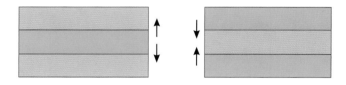

3 Now cut each of the assembled strip units into five 2½in segments.

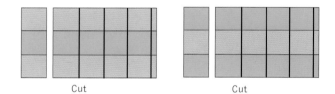

Cut   Cut

4 Assemble and sew the three nine-patch blocks as shown, pinning at every seam intersection to make sure that the seams are neatly aligned. Press the work. Put the spare unit to one side.

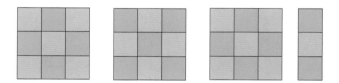

5 Repeat with all seven pairs of strips to make twenty nine-patch blocks. Unpick four of the spare units to give you the ten extra 2½in squares required to add to your other squares.

ASSEMBLING THE BLOCKS

6 Working with one pile of 2½in x 6½in rectangles allocated for the frames, take one 2½in sashing fabric square and lay it right sides together on a 2½in x 6½in rectangle. Sew across the diagonal. If it helps, draw the diagonal line in first or make a fold to mark your stitching line. Flip the square over and press towards the light fabric. Trim the excess light fabric but do not trim the 2½in x 6½in rectangle. Although this creates a little more bulk, it helps to keep your work in shape.

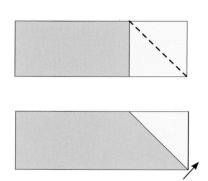

7 Take another 2½in light square and sew it to the other side as shown, pressing and trimming as before. Make four of these units.

Make 4

8 Sew two of these units to each side of one of the nine-patch units. Press as shown.

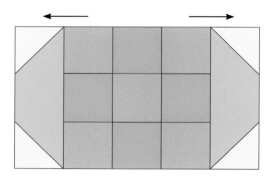

9 Sew a coloured 2½in square to each side of the remaining two units. Press as shown.

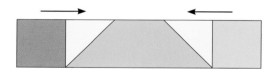

10 Sew to the top and bottom of the nine-patch unit, pinning at every seam intersection to ensure a perfect match. Press the work. Repeat to make twenty blocks.

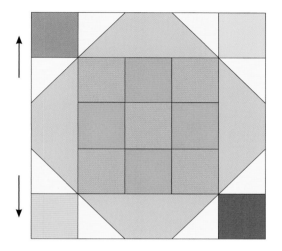

ASSEMBLING THE QUILT

11 Create the first row by sewing a 2½in square to the left-hand side of four 2½in x 10½in sashing rectangles. Sew together and then sew a 2½in square to the right-hand side of the last rectangle. Press towards the sashing squares. Make six of these rows.

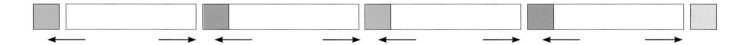

12 Create the second row by sewing a 2½in x 10½in sashing rectangle to the left-hand side of four blocks. Sew together and then sew a sashing rectangle to the right-hand side of the last block. Press the work. Make five of these rows.

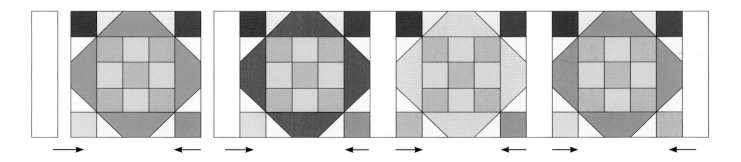

13 Referring to the diagram below, sew the rows together, pinning at every seam intersection to ensure a perfect match. Press the work.

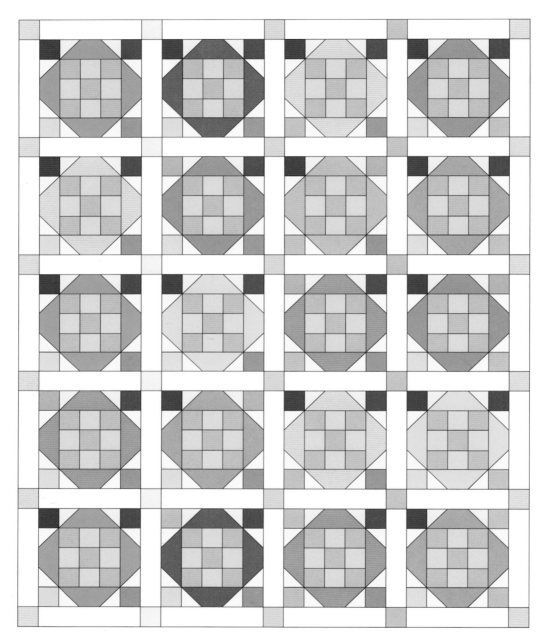

14 Your quilt top is now complete. Quilt as desired and bind to finish – see Quilting and Binding a Quilt.

If you wish to create a scrappy binding cut each of the six binding strips into rectangles approximately 2½in x 10½in. Sew them into a continuous length making sure you don't put fabric from the same strip next to each other.

You can never go wrong with a blue and white quilt and for our variation we chose to use a blue jelly roll combined with a tone-on-tone white fabric. The quilt was made by Kath Bock and longarm quilted by The Quilt Room.

FANTASY FLOWERS

We had a lot of fun creating this gorgeous quilt. We decided on our central flowers quite easily but then had to work out how to create a border within the block formation. Choosing a smaller outer flower block allowed us to design a sawtooth border within the flower block, which sets off the quilt beautifully. We then set the quilt on point and hey presto, a dynamic and interesting design! The jelly roll fabrics we used were very adaptable and would easily have created a much brighter quilt just by changing the additional fabrics used.

This jelly roll, in a fabric range called Lovely from Sandy Gervais, had a bright mix of aqua, peach and yellow together with some delicious light strips. We chose a pale green and yellow for our additional fabrics as we wanted to create a soft and gentle quilt.

Fantasy Flowers Quilt

Vital Statistics

Finished Size:	57in x 57in
Block Size:	8in
Blocks per Quilt:	40 blocks (24 inner flower and 16 outer flower, which includes sawtooth border)
Setting:	On point

Requirements

- One jelly roll OR forty 2½in strips cut across the width of the fabric
- 1¾yd (1.5m) of green background fabric
- 16in (40cm) of yellow fabric for setting triangles
- Binding from jelly roll strips
- Multi-Size 45/90 ruler or other speciality ruler for making half-square and quarter-square triangles

SORTING YOUR STRIPS

- Eight yellow strips for inner flower blocks.
- Four peach strips for inner flower blocks.
- Seven aqua strips for outer flower blocks.
- Nine light strips for outer flower blocks and sawtooth border.
- Four rust strips for sawtooth border.
- Six strips for the binding. Two are spare.

CUTTING INSTRUCTIONS

Jelly roll strips – Yellow:
- Cut each of the eight strips in half to create two rectangles approximately 2½in x 21in. Keep the two strips from each pair together.

Peach:
- Cut each strip in half to create two rectangles approximately 2½in x 21in. You need eight.

Aqua:
- Cut four aqua strips into sixteen 2½in squares. You need sixty-four for the outer flower blocks.
- Leave the three remaining aqua strips uncut.

Light:
- Take two light strips and cut each into sixteen 2½in squares. You need thirty-two.
- Leave the remaining seven light strips uncut.

Green background fabric:
- Cut sixteen strips 2½in wide across the fabric width.
- Take twelve of these strips and subcut each into eight rectangles 2½in x 4½in. You need ninety-six.
- Cut the remaining four strips in half to create two rectangles 2½in x 21in. You need eight.
- Cut one strip 14in wide and subcut into three 14in squares. Cut across both diagonals to make twelve setting triangles.

Additional yellow fabric:
- Cut one strip 14in wide and subcut into two 14in squares. Cut across both diagonals to create eight setting triangles. Cutting this way ensures there are no bias edges.

MAKING THE INNER FLOWER BLOCKS

1 Working with one pair of yellow strips at a time, take one yellow 2½in x 21in rectangle and one background green 2½in x 21in rectangle and press right sides together, ensuring they are exactly one on top of the other. Pressing will help hold the strips together.

2 Lay them out on a cutting mat and position the Multi-Size 45/90 ruler as shown, lining up the 2in mark at the bottom edge of the strips. Trim the selvedge and cut the first triangle. The cut out triangle has a flat top, which would have been a dog ear you needed to cut off, so it is saving you time.

2in line

3 Rotate the Multi-Size 45/90 ruler 180 degrees as shown and cut the next triangle. Continue along the strip to cut twelve triangles.

2in line

4 Sew along the diagonals to form twelve half-square triangle units. Trim all dog ears and press open with the seams pressed towards the darker fabric.

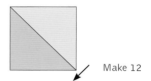

Make 12

5 Repeat steps 1–4 with the other yellow rectangle from the pair and a peach 2½in x 21in rectangle to make twelve half-square triangle units. Press towards the darker fabric.

Make 12

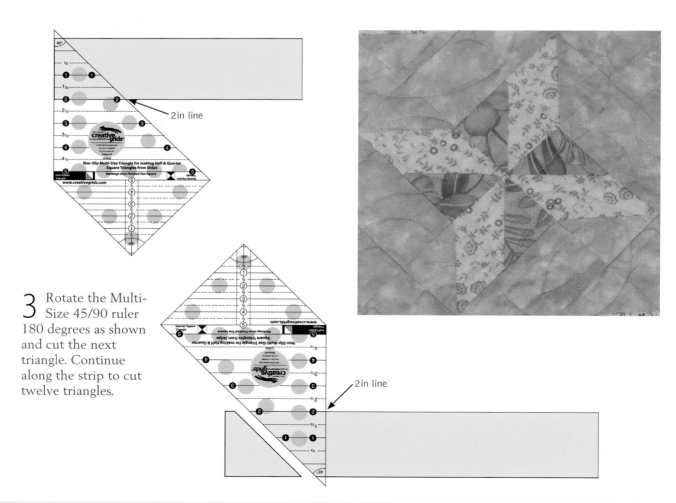

6 Join a yellow and green half-square triangle unit to a yellow and peach half-square triangle unit as shown. Now sew a green 2½in x 4½in rectangle to the left-hand side. Press the work. Make twelve units.

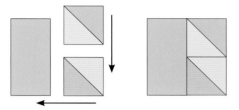

Make 12

7 Sew four units together as shown, rotating each unit 90 degrees to the right. Pin at every seam intersection to ensure a perfect match. Make three inner flower blocks.

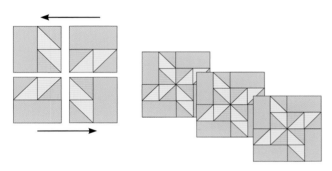

8 Using the remaining seven pairs of yellow 2½in x 21in rectangles, the remaining seven peach 2½in x 21in rectangles and the remaining seven green background 2½in x 21in rectangles, repeat the above steps to make a total of twenty-four inner flower blocks.

MAKING THE OUTER FLOWER BLOCKS

9 Take one aqua and one light jelly roll strip and press right sides together, ensuring that they are exactly one on top of the other.

10 Lay them out on a cutting mat and position the Multi-Size 45/90 as shown in the diagram, lining up the 2in mark at the bottom edge of the strips. Trim the selvedge and cut the first triangle.

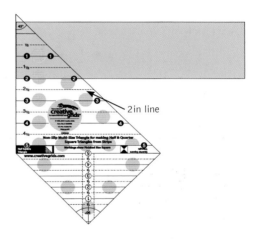

2in line

11 Rotate the Multi-Size 45/90 ruler 180 degrees to the right as shown and cut the next triangle. Continue along the strip to cut twenty-four triangles.

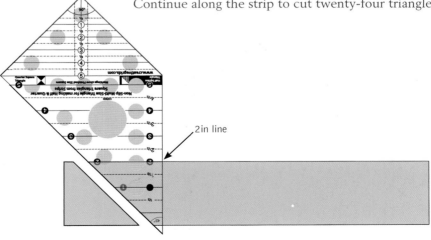

2in line

12 Sew along the diagonals to form twenty-four half-square triangle units. Trim all dog ears and press seams towards the darker fabric. Repeat with two other aqua and light strips to form sixty-four half-square triangle units in total. Eight are spare.

Make 64

13 Repeat steps 9–12 using four light and four rust jelly roll strips. You need ninety-six in total.

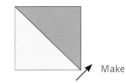

Make 96

14 Sew an aqua and light half-square triangle unit to both sides of an aqua 2½in square. Press as shown. Make two of these units.

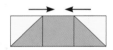

15 Sew a 2½in aqua square to both sides of a 2½in light square. Press as shown.

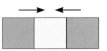

16 Sew the rows together pinning at every seam intersection to ensure a perfect match. Press the work. We used the same fabric for the squares in each block and the same half-square triangle units but you can make them as scrappy as you like.

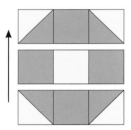

17 Sew three light and rust half-square triangle units together as shown and sew a further three light and rust half-square triangle units together with a light square on the left-hand side. Press the work.

18 Sew the set of three to the left side of the block as shown. Press the work. Sew the set of four to the top. Press the work. Repeat to make sixteen outer flower blocks.

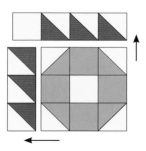

ASSEMBLING THE QUILT

19 Referring to the quilt diagram below, lay out the blocks and setting triangles and when happy with the layout, create row 1 by sewing two outer flower blocks together and sewing a yellow setting triangle to both ends. The setting triangles have been cut slightly larger to make the blocks 'float', so when sewing the setting triangles make sure the bottom of the triangle is aligned with the block.

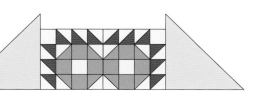

20 Create row 2 by sewing an outer flower block to each side of two inner flower blocks with a green setting triangle unit to both ends. Continue sewing the rows together with the correct colour setting triangle at each end, pressing rows in alternate directions. Sew the rows together pinning at every seam intersection to ensure a perfect match.

21 Lastly, sew two green setting triangles together to form a corner triangle. Make four and and sew these to each corner. Press the work.

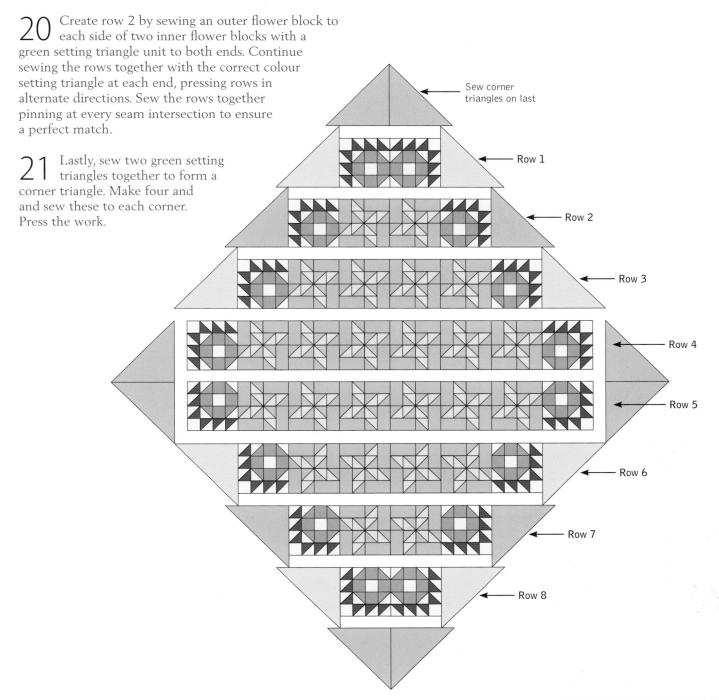

Sew corner triangles on last

Row 1

Row 2

Row 3

Row 4

Row 5

Row 6

Row 7

Row 8

22 Your quilt top is now complete. Quilt as desired and bind to finish – see Quilting and Binding a Quilt.

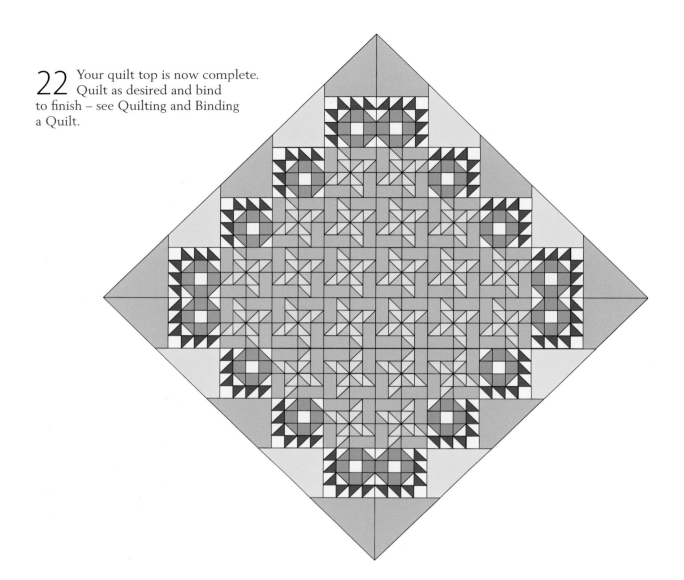

Our variation was made using a jelly roll of civil war reproduction fabrics. For our additional fabric we used yellow and pink reproduction fabrics, which gave us an authentic-looking civil war quilt. We varied the sawtooth border slightly from the instructions to show how you can play around with the placement of units to create different effects.

General Techniques

TOOLS

All the projects in this book require rotary cutting equipment. You will need a self-healing cutting mat at least 18in x 24in and a rotary cutter. We recommend the 45mm or the 60mm diameter rotary cutter. Any rotary cutting work requires rulers and most people have a make they prefer. We like the Creative Grids rulers as their markings are clear, they do not slip on fabric and their Turn-a-Round facility is so useful when dealing with half-inch measurements. We recommend the 6½in x 24in as a basic ruler plus a large square no less than 12½in, which is handy for squaring up and making sure you are always cutting at right angles.

We have tried not to use too many different speciality rulers but when working with 2½in strips you do have to re-think some cutting procedures. You do need a speciality ruler to cut half-square triangles in the Fantasy Flowers quilt. Creative Grids have designed the Multi-Size 45/90 ruler for us, which enables you to cut both half-square and quarter-square triangles. Whichever ruler you decide to use, please make sure you are lining up your work on the correct markings.

BASIC TOOL KIT

- Tape measure
- Rotary cutter
- Cutting ruler
- Cutting mat
- Needles
- Pins
- Scissors
- Pencil
- Fabric marker
- Iron
- Sewing machine

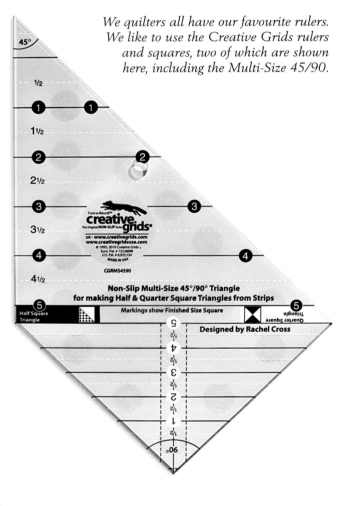

We quilters all have our favourite rulers. We like to use the Creative Grids rulers and squares, two of which are shown here, including the Multi-Size 45/90.

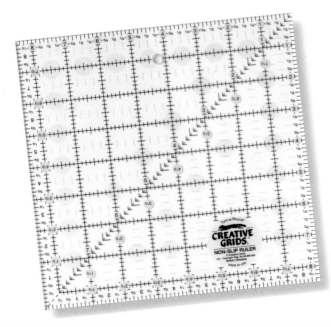

ROTARY CUTTING

Always take great care when using rotary cutting equipment as the blades are razor sharp. These instructions are for a right-handed person – reverse if you are left-handed.

1 Before cutting fabric with a rotary cutter the edge of the fabric must be straightened. Fold the fabric in half, selvedge to selvedge, and place the ruler along the right edge of the fabric, making sure one of the horizontal lines marked on the ruler is aligned with the fold of the fabric. This will ensure you are cutting at a right angle to the fold.

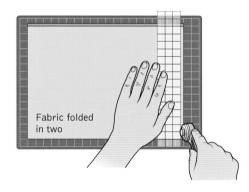

Fabric folded in two

2 Hold the ruler firmly with your left hand, positioning your thumb at the bottom of the ruler and your fingers stretching up the ruler. Hold the cutter in your right hand (if right-handed).

3 Keeping the blade against the edge of the ruler, push the cutter away from your body, stopping when the blade is even with your fingertips. Without lifting the cutter from the fabric, move the thumb on the ruler up to your fingertips and then move your fingertips up the ruler – walking your hand up the ruler while you continue cutting. Cutting this way will ensure you always have good pressure on your ruler so it will not slip.

4 Rotate the mat so that the ruler can still be held firmly with the left hand. You are now ready to cut strips, moving from left to right across the fabric. It is good

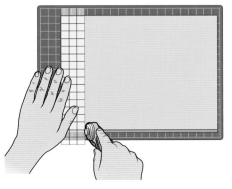

practice to check that you are still cutting at a right angle after every four or five cuts. If you start cutting away from the right angle you will find that V-shapes will appear at the fold when your strip is opened out.

SEAMS

We cannot stress enough the importance of maintaining an accurate ¼in seam allowance throughout. We prefer to say an accurate *scant* ¼in seam because there are two factors to take into consideration. Firstly, the thickness of thread and secondly when you press your seam allowance to one side, it takes up a tiny amount of fabric. These are both extremely small amounts but if they are ignored you will find your *exact* ¼in seam allowance is taking up more than ¼in.

SEAM ALLOWANCE TEST

It is well worth testing your seam allowance before starting on a quilt and most sewing machines have various needle positions which can be used to make any adjustments.

Take a 2½in strip and cut off three segments 1½in wide (diagram A). Sew two segments together down the longer side and press seam to one side (B). Sew the third segment across the top. It should fit exactly (C). If it doesn't, you need to make an adjustment to your seam allowance. If it is too long, your seam allowance is too wide and can be corrected by moving the needle on your sewing machine to the right. If it is too small, your seam allowance is too narrow and this can be corrected by moving the needle to the left.

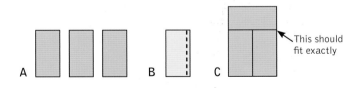

A   B   C   This should fit exactly

PRESSING

In quiltmaking, pressing is of vital importance and if extra care is taken you will be well rewarded. This is especially true when dealing with strips. If your strips start bowing and stretching you will lose accuracy.

- Always set your seam after sewing by pressing the seam as sewn, without opening up your strips. This eases any tension and prevents the seam line from distorting. Move the iron with an up and down motion, zigzagging along the seam rather than ironing down the length, which could cause distortion.

- Open up your strips and press on the *right* side of the fabric towards the darker fabric, if necessary guiding the seam underneath to make sure it is going in the right direction. Press with an up and down motion rather than along the length of the strip.

- Always take care if using steam and certainly don't use steam anywhere near a bias edge.
- When you are joining more than two strips together, press the seams after attaching *each* strip. You are far more likely to get bowing if you leave it until your strip unit is complete before pressing.
- Each seam must be pressed flat before another seam is sewn across it. Unless there is a special reason for not doing so, seams are pressed towards the darker fabric. The main criteria when joining seams is to have the seam allowances going in the opposite direction to each other as they then nest together without bulk. Your patchwork will lie flat and your seam intersections will be accurate.

PINNING

Don't underestimate the benefits of pinning. When you have to align a seam it is important to insert pins to stop any movement when sewing. Long, fine pins with flat heads are recommended as they will go through fabric layers easily and allow you to sew up to and over them.

Seams should always be pressed in opposite directions so they will nest together. Insert a pin at right angles or diagonally through the seam intersection ensuring that the seams are matching perfectly. When sewing, do not remove the pin too early as the fabric might shift and seams will not be perfectly aligned.

CHAIN PIECING

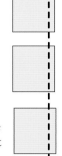

Chain piecing is the technique of feeding a series of pieces through the sewing machine without lifting the presser foot and without cutting the thread between each piece. Always chain piece when you can – it saves time and thread. Once your chain is complete simply snip the thread between the pieces.

When chain piecing shapes other than squares and rectangles it is sometimes preferable when finishing one shape, to lift the presser foot slightly and reposition on the next shape, still leaving the thread uncut.

REMOVING DOG EARS

A dog ear is the excess piece of fabric that overlaps past the seam allowance when sewing triangles to other shapes. Dog ears should always be cut off to reduce bulk. They can be trimmed using a rotary cutter although snipping with small scissors is quicker. Ensure you are trimming the points parallel to the straight edge of the triangle.

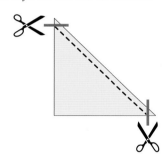

JOINING BORDER AND BINDING STRIPS

If you need to join strips for your borders and binding, you may choose to join them with a diagonal seam to make them less noticeable (diagram A). Press the seams open (B).

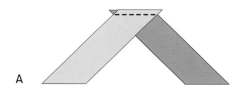

A

B

ADDING BORDERS

The fabric requirements in this book all assume you are going to be sewing straight rather than mitred borders. If you intend to have mitred borders you will need to add sufficient fabric for this.

ADDING STRAIGHT BORDERS

1 Determine the vertical measurement from top to bottom through the centre of your quilt top (A). Cut two side border strips to this measurement. Mark the halves and quarters of one quilt side and one border with pins. Placing right sides together and matching the pins, stitch quilt and border together, easing the quilt side to fit where necessary. Repeat on the opposite side (B). Press open.

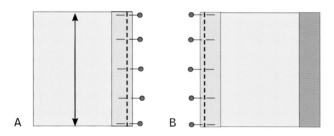

2 Determine the horizontal measurement from side to side across the centre of the quilt top (C). Cut two top and bottom border strips to this measurement and add to the quilt top in the same manner.

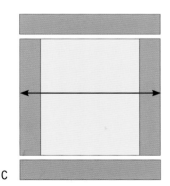

ADDING MITRED BORDERS

1 Measure the length and width of the quilt and cut two border strips the length of the quilt plus twice the width of the border and cut two border strips the width of the quilt plus twice the width of the border.

2 Sew the border strips to the quilt starting and ending ¼in away from corners, backstitching to secure at either end. Begin sewing right next to where you finished sewing the previous border but ensure the stitching doesn't overlap. When all borders are sewn, press and lay the quilt on a flat surface, reverse side up.

3 Fold the top border up and align it with the side border. Press the 45 degree line that starts at the ¼in stop and runs to the outside border edge (A).

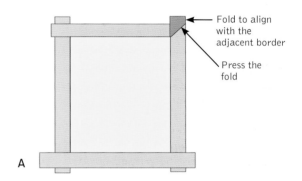

Fold to align with the adjacent border

Press the fold

4 Now lift the side border above the top border and fold it to align with the top border. Press it to create a 45 degree line (B). Repeat with all four corners.

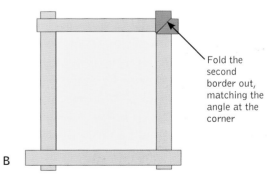

Fold the second border out, matching the angle at the corner

5 Align the horizontal and vertical borders in one corner by folding the quilt diagonally and stitch along the pressed 45 degree line to form the mitre, backstitching at either end. Trim excess border fabric ¼in from the sewn line. Repeat with the other corners.

QUILTING

Quilting stitches hold the patchwork top, wadding (batting) and backing together and create texture over your finished patchwork. The choice is yours whether you hand quilt, machine quilt or send it off to a longarm quilting service. There are many books dedicated to the techniques of hand and machine quilting but the basic procedure is as follows.

1 With the aid of templates or a ruler, mark out the quilting lines on the patchwork top.

2 Cut the backing and wadding at least 3in larger all around than the patchwork top. Pin or tack (baste) the layers together to prepare them for quilting.

3 Quilt either by hand or by machine. When all quilting is finished remove tacking, pins and any marking lines.

BINDING A QUILT

The fabric requirements in this book are for a 2½in double-fold French binding cut on the straight of grain.

1 Trim the excess backing and wadding so that the edges are even with the top of the quilt.

2 Join your binding strips into a continuous length, making sure there is sufficient to go around the quilt plus 8in–10in for the corners and overlapping ends. With wrong sides together, press the binding in half lengthways. Fold and press under ½in to neaten the edge at the end where you will start sewing.

3 On the right side of the quilt and starting about 12in away from a corner, align the edges of the double thickness binding with the edge of the quilt so that the cut edges are towards the edges of the quilt and pin to hold in place. Sew with a ¼in seam allowance, leaving the first inch open.

4 At the first corner, stop ¼in from the edge of the fabric and backstitch (diagram A). Lift the needle and foot and fold the binding upwards (B). Now fold the binding downwards (C). Stitch from the edge to ¼in from the next corner and repeat the turn. Continue around the quilt working each corner the same way.

5 When you arrive back at the starting point, cut the binding, fold under the cut edge and overlap at the starting point.

6 Fold over the binding to the back of the quilt and hand stitch in place, folding the binding at each corner to form a neat mitre.

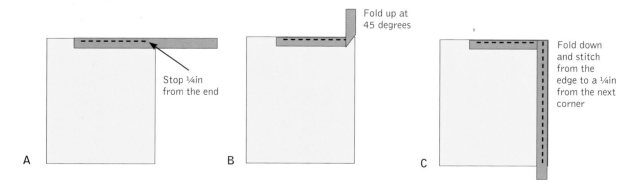

MAKING A LARGER QUILT

If you want to make a larger version of any of the quilts in the book, refer to the Vital Statistics of the quilt which shows the block size, the number of blocks, how the blocks are set plus the size of border used. You can then calculate your requirements for a larger quilt.

SETTING ON POINT

Any block can take on a totally new look when set on point and you might like to try one of the quilts to see what it looks like on point. Some people are a little daunted as there are a few points to take into consideration but here is all you need to know.

How wide will my blocks be when set on point?

To calculate the measurement of the block from point to point multiply the size of the finished block by 1.414. Example: a 12in block will measure 12in x 1.414 which is 16.97in – just under 17in. Now you can calculate how many blocks you need for your quilt.

How do I piece blocks on point?

Piece rows diagonally, starting at a corner. Triangles have to be added to the end of each row before joining the rows and these are called setting triangles.

How do I calculate what size setting triangles to cut?

Setting triangles form the outside of your quilt and need to have the straight of grain on the outside edge to prevent stretching. To ensure this, these triangles are formed from quarter-square triangles, i.e., a square cut into four. The measurement for this is: diagonal block size + 1¼in.

Example: a 12in block (diagonal measurement approx. 17in) should be 18¼in.

Corners triangles are added last. They also need to have the outside edge on the straight of grain so these should be cut from half-square triangles. To calculate the size of square to cut in half, divide the finished size of your block by 1.414 and then add ⅞in.

Example: a 12in block would be 12in divided by 1.414 = 8.49in + ⅞in (0.88) = 9.37in (or 9½in as it can be trimmed later).

Most diagonal quilts start off with one block and in each row and thereafter the number of blocks increases by two. All rows contain an odd number of blocks. To calculate the finished size of the quilt, count the number of diagonals across and multiply this by the diagonal measurement of the block. Do the same with the number of blocks down and multiply this by the diagonal measurement of the block.

If you want a rectangular quilt instead of a square one, count the number of blocks in the row that establishes the width and repeat that number in following rows until the desired length is established.

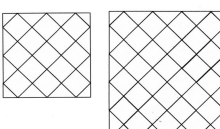

This row establishes width of quilt

Repeat row

Repeat row

CALCULATING BACKING FABRIC

The patterns in this book do not include fabric requirements for backing as many people like to use extra wide backing fabric so they do not have to have any joins.

USING 60in WIDE FABRIC

This is a simple calculation as to how much fabric you will need to buy.

Example: your quilt is 54in x 72in. Your backing needs to be 3in larger all round so your backing measurement is 60in x 78in. If you have found 60in wide backing, then you would buy the length which is 78in. However, if you have found 90in wide backing, you can turn it round and you would only have to buy the width of 60in.

USING 42in WIDE FABRIC

You will need to have a join or joins in order to get the required measurement unless the backing measurement for your quilt is 42in or less on one side. If your backing measurement is less than 42in then you need only buy one length.

Using the previous example, if your backing measurement is 60in x 78in, you will have to have one seam somewhere in your backing. If you join two lengths of 42in fabric together your new fabric measurement will be 84in (less a little for the seam). This would be sufficient for the length of your quilt so you need to buy twice the width, i.e. 60in x 2 = 120in. Your seam will run horizontal.

If your quilt length is more than your new backing fabric measurement of 84in you will need to use the measurement of 84in for the width of your quilt and you will have to buy twice the length. Your seam will then run vertical.

LABELLING YOUR QUILT

When you have finished your quilt it is important to label it even if the information you put on the label is just your name and the date. When looking at antique quilts it is always interesting to piece together information about the quilt, so you can be sure that any extra information you put on the label will be of immense interest to quilters of the future. For example, you could say why you made the quilt and who it was for, or for what special occasion.

Labels can be as ornate as you like, but a very simple and quick method is to write on a piece of calico with a permanent marker pen and then appliqué this to the back of your quilt.

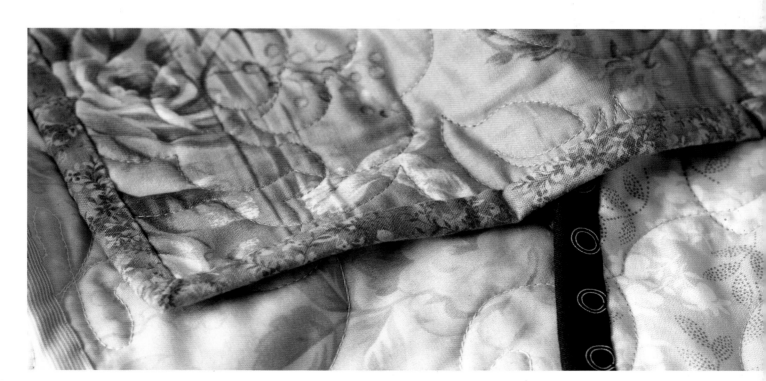

About the Authors

Pam Lintott opened her shop, The Quilt Room, in 1981, which she still runs today, along with her daughter Nicky. Pam is the author of *The Quilt Room Patchwork & Quilting Workshops*, as well as *The Quilter's Workbook*. Nicky has the added responsibility of looking after Freddie who is now 18 months old and has quickly learned that the sorting of jelly roll strips is great fun!

The Quilt Room is housed in a 15th century inn, located in the historic market town of Dorking, Surrey. When you enter the shop through the doors marked 'Public Bar' they know their customers are only too pleased to be confronted by bolts of fabric and jelly rolls rather than caskets of ale!

More Layer Cake, Jelly Roll and Charm Quilts is Pam and Nicky's sixth book for David & Charles following on from *Jelly Roll Sampler Quilts*, *Two from One Jelly Roll Quilts*, *Jelly Roll Inspirations*, *Layer Cake, Jelly Roll & Charm Quilts* and their phenomenally successful *Jelly Roll Quilts*.

Acknowledgments

Pam and Nicky would firstly like to thank Mark Dunn at Moda for his continued support and for allowing them to use the names jelly roll and layer cake in the title and throughout the book. Thanks also go to Lissa Alexander and the team at Moda, with special thanks to Susan Rogers who always takes such good care of them.

Their thanks also go to the loyal team of staff at The Quilt Room who keep The Quilt Room running smoothly when Pam and Nicky are rushing to meet tight deadlines.

Thanks also go to the lovely ladies in Cornwall who are always ready to assist when time is short, with special thanks to Ellen Seward, Kath Bock and Vivian de Lang.

Last but not least, special thanks to Pam's husband Nick and to Nicky's husband Rob for looking after sheep, chickens, guinea fowl, dogs and one very active toddler who might not otherwise get fed!

Useful Contacts

The Quilt Room
Shop and Mail Order
37–39 High Street,
Dorking,
Surrey, RH4 1AR, UK
Tel: 01306 877307
www.quiltroom.co.uk

Moda Fabrics/United Notions
13800 Hutton Drive,
Dallas, Texas 75234, USA
Tel: 800-527-9447
www.modafabrics.com

Winbourne Fabrics Ltd
(Moda's UK Distributor)
Unit 3A, Forge Way,
Knypersley,
Stoke on Trent ST8 7DN, UK

Creative Grids (UK) Limited
Unit 1J, Peckleton Lane
Business Park,
Peckleton Lane, Peckleton,
Leicester LE9 7RN, UK
Tel: 01455 828667
www.creativegrids.com

Janome UK Ltd
Janome Centre, Southside,
Stockport,
Cheshire SK6 2SP, UK
Tel: 0161 666 6011
www.janome.com

Index